Mississippi Writers Talking

VOLUME II

Mississippi Writers Talking

VOLUME II

INTERVIEWS WITH

Walker Percy

Ellen Douglas

Willie Morris

Margaret Walker Alexander

James Whitehead

Turner Cassity

John Griffin Jones
Interviewer

UNIVERSITY PRESS OF MISSISSIPPI / JACKSON

6/1984.
am. Lit.

This volume is sponsored by the
Mississippi Department of Archives and History

Library of Congress Cataloging in Publication Data (Revised)
Main entry under title:

Mississippi writers talking.

  Sponsored by the Department of Archives and History"
—T.p. verso.
    1. Authors, American—Mississippi—Interviews.
2. Authors, American—20th century—Interviews.
3. American fiction—20th century—History and criti-
cism—Addresses, essays, lectures.   4. Mississippi—
Social Life and customs—Addresses, essays, lectures.
I. Jones, John G.   II. Welty, Eudora, 1909–
III. Mississippi. Dept of Archives and History.
PS266.M7M5   810'.9'9762   81-23057
ISBN 0-87805-174-0 (v. 2)
ISBN 0-87805-175-9 (pbk. : v. 2)

Contents

Foreword

This second volume of the two-volume work, *Mississippi Writers Talking*, continues and concludes the series of interviews with Mississippi writers conducted by John Jones when he was oral historian with the Mississippi Department of Archives and History (1979–1981). Interviews with Eudora Welty, Shelby Foote, Elizabeth Spencer, Barry Hannah, and Beth Henley appeared in the first volume. This second volume includes interviews with Walker Percy, Ellen Douglas, Willie Morris, Margaret Walker Alexander, James Whitehead, and Turner Cassity.

Standard methodology of oral history was used in collecting the interviews. The interviews are printed here almost exactly as they appear in the transcriptions on file in the Department of Archives and History. Each author has had an opportunity to review the transcript of his or her interview, and some editorial deletions were necessary because of space limitations. Otherwise, the conversations are as tape recorded and constitute an exceptionally interesting source for the study of Mississippi's literary and cultural history.

Appreciation is due the Board of Trustees of the Department of Archives and History for their decision to sponsor this two-volume set. I would also like to thank the Department's Information and Education staff for overseeing the project; the University Press for a most pleasant working relationship; and John Griffin Jones for his persistence and talent in producing eleven lively conversations with eleven renowned Mississippians.

Elbert R. Hilliard, *Director*
Mississippi Department of Archives and History

Mississippi Writers Talking

VOLUME II

Photograph by John Griffin Jones

Walker Percy

April 17, 1980

What do you ask a man who once wrote, in response to
the lack of creativity on the part of his interviewers, an
article entitled "Questions They Never Ask Me: A Self-
Interview"? Obviously he'd already asked, and answered, many of the questions pertinent to his fiction.
Undaunted, I appealed to him in early 1980. He kindly
consented to be interviewed, and his letter said to meet
him at a restaurant in Mandeville, Louisiana, on the
shores of Lake Pontchartrain, for lunch, and then we
would drive to his home in Covington for the interview. Because the spring floods of the Pearl River had
covered my rural route to the south, I had to double
back through Jackson, which made me an agonizing
hour late for our appointment. When I ran up to the
restaurant, he was the first person I saw, talking quietly
with a group of young people. Too late to feel nervous
about intruding on their conversation, I introduced myself. I was greeted warmly—especially by Percy, who
wore a nylon parka over a white shirt, corduroy trou-
sers, and running shoes. He was taller than I'd imagined, with the quick, nimble movements of a boy. We
had a light lunch of gumbo and bread, and when someone noticed it was three o'clock, the regular group

promptly dispersed. Outside, he pointed to his little blue pickup and warned me, "You better stick to my tail if you can. I drive pretty fast." He did, and in no time, it seems, we were on the back porch of his house—overlooking a stretch of bayou—drinking iced tea and talking.

Jones: This is John Jones with the Mississippi Department of Archives and History. Dr. Percy, I wanted to start off with your giving us a little of your early background if you would.

Percy: I was born in Birmingham, Alabama, May 28, 1916. My father was named LeRoy Percy. He was a first cousin of William Alexander Percy. He married Martha Susan Phinizy from Athens, Georgia. His father was a Walker Percy, one of the three brothers—- Walker, Senator LeRoy Percy, and William Percy from Memphis. They all started out in Greenville. LeRoy, Senator Percy, stayed in Greenville, and William and Walker went to seek their fortunes elsewhere. Walker went to Birmingham, which was a new city.

Jones: Right. And William Alexander Percy says in *Lanterns on the Levee* that the three came back together during the Senator's race against Vardaman.

Percy: Right. I think they did.

Jones: Did you ever come to know or did you ever meet the Senator?

Percy: Once. It was very brief, but I remember it very distinctly. I don't think either one of my brothers recalls ever meeting him; maybe they didn't. I remember once he was passing through Birmingham. He was a great friend of my father; they got along well. Uncle LeRoy and my father were great hunting companions. They both would come down to New Orleans and play poker at the Boston Club and go hunting at the Lake Arthur Duck Club. It must have been shortly before my father's death, which was in 1929. This must have

been the late '20s—'26, '27, '28. Senator Percy was
passing through Birmingham, and I remember very
distinctly going down with my father to the L & N
railroad station. I remember exactly where it was. The
train only stopped for a few minutes, so there was only
time enough for Senator Percy to get off the train and
stand on the siding. We talked to him a few minutes
before he got back on the train. I'm trying to figure out
where he'd been and where he was going. He was
dressed in a very light tropical suit. He was very fit and
small, smaller than I expected. He was a very handsome
and trim figure of a man with a white mustache, very
erect and rather imperial looking. He stood on the
platform and talked to my father. I can't remember
what we talked about, but after a few minutes he got
on the train and went on. He must have come in from
Florida going back to Greenville, but how? I don't
know. The L & N—maybe he was going to Memphis.
It couldn't have been long before his death. I've forgotten when he died, '27, '28?

Jones: Christmas Eve of '29.

Percy: '29. Hm. So it must have been '28.

Jones: It's always been my idea and one of the reasons
I started this project, that if the Senator had been successful in the election—that Will so skillfully described
in *Lanterns*—that maybe we would have been saved
from the tradition of the demagogues.

Percy: Well, maybe so, but I doubt it. I can't think of
a state where it happened, where comparable people
were successful. I think it was probably a historical
tide. The quasi-populists, a funny combination of
populism and racism, were bound to win. I don't see it
so much in personal terms as that. I think the same
thing happened in Alabama; the same thing happened
in Georgia. I think if R. E. Lee himself had been
running, it wouldn't have made that much difference.

Jones: I know Shelby Foote has said that growing up

in Greenville the Senator was for his people the shining knight on a white horse, but that now he's not even sure that Bilbo didn't have the people's interests closer to heart.

Percy: Well, it depends. In a way Bilbo was a populist, I guess. Maybe he did; although as a populist he was corrupted and finally totally corrupt. Uncle LeRoy maybe had a streak of paternalism in him, not only as applied to black people, but also maybe to white people. But within that framework he wanted to do what was best for what he called "his people." It certainly was not in the liberal framework that we're familiar with. God knows Vardaman and Bilbo were not either. But I would disagree with Shelby saying that the Senator did not have the best interests of his people, as he saw it, in mind. Maybe nowadays we look on that as being too paternalistic. We would think maybe he was too much of an aristocrat who thought he knew what was best for blacks and whites, poor whites. But I think he was out to do the best he could within his own lights, within his own frame of reference.

Jones: Right. Do you feel that the planter, the aristocrat, is the one to blame for the way that things developed in the Delta and the South? Do you think he was the real villain feeding the people false information and leading them on with the promise of upward mobility if they performed well and were good like him?

Percy: You mean black people?

Jones: Whites too. Do you see the planter as the scamp?

Percy: No more so than other white people. I don't necessarily indict them so much as think they were the victims of history, the victims of bad luck. That's the way I like to think of it. I think the bad luck came to pass when the cotton gin was developed and cotton became profitable and therefore slavery became profitable. You had this tremendous profit motive.

When you say aristocrats, you know, that's a very
tricky term. Who's an aristocrat? In the South it means
somebody who's had the plantation more than a couple
of generations. It was bad luck. You had these people
who were making a lot of money and, you know, con-
sidering the human condition, the temptation was too
much. It was too easy to make money. Slavery was
profitable here, not in Massachusetts. It meant that
whoever could get slaves got slaves. After the thing
started, here again the temptation was too great. I remember my uncle Will Percy defending the plantation,
the sharecropper system, saying it could work out very
equitably. After the Civil War the blacks had nothing;
the whites had nothing except the land; so therefore the
white planters proposed to share their land and share
half the produce. It sounds very good except that what
with the human condition, it depended on a man being
a good man for it to work out justly. Some people were
good, and maybe most were not. It meant that it was
too easy, too damn easy to exploit the blacks. When it's
that easy, you do it, most people do it. I don't single
out the planter class as being any more exploitative
than any other white class, except that they were in a
position to do it. Of course, traditionally it was the
middle class, white middle class, who were rougher on
the blacks than the planter class. It was Simon Legree's
class . . .

Jones: The Snopes.

Percy: . . . you know, who were always tougher on the
blacks than ole white massah.

Jones: I know in *Lanterns on the Levee* that Will says his
father became one of his chief delights after he learned a
little sense. Do you remember any of the stories that
your Uncle Will might have told you when you were
growing up about any of those old battles?

Percy: Well, to tell you the truth, I've got the stories
so confused in my mind with *Lanterns on the Levee*. The

stories that he used to tell us are the same ones that you
read in *Lanterns on the Levee*, about the famous confrontation with Bilbo in the—I think it was in the coffee
shop of which hotel in Jackson, Robert E. Lee? During
the campaign. I think it was my grandfather who came
into the hotel with my uncle and Senator Percy and saw
Bilbo sitting there and referred to him as "that no-good
son of a bitch," or some such words. I can't remember,
as I say, if I read this or remember the story which he
told several times, that Bilbo never looked up from
eating his oatmeal. He went on eating. I think Shelby
has been seduced a little bit by the romanticism of
populism. He likes to think of Bilbo as a man of the
people. Bilbo was, as my grandfather said, "a no-good
son of a bitch!" If you want to record this for your
history, you can do it. He was totally corrupt and
didn't give a damn about the people. Maybe at the
beginning he did, but, unlike Huey Long, who did
care about the people in the beginning, I never really
saw any signs that Bilbo did.
Jones: "A self-accused bribe-taker," as Will Percy said.
Percy: Yes.
Jones: I think one of the interesting things that turns
up in your work is something that, again, Will had in
Lanterns on the Levee concerning the Senator's attitude
after he lost the Senate race in 1912. The Senator said
in a letter he wrote to a fellow in Winona that shooting
for the stars has always been pretty poor marksmanship,
it seemed to him, and he came later in his life to decide
that a man had to be as good a man as he could be in
his own little postage stamp corner of the world.
Percy: Yes.
Jones: I know Will Barrett in *The Last Gentleman* tells
Sutter after Jamie dies that he ought to come back to
the South and make a contribution, however small. Did
you draw that parallel consciously? Did you have that
in mind?

Percy: Yes, I had it in mind. That's pretty close reading. Nobody, I think, has ever picked up on that before.

Jones: Well, I think it turns up in other places too.

Percy: Yes.

Jones: Tom More in *Love in the Ruins* has the secret to save the world with his lapsometer, and yet he is determined to stay with his three girls in the hotel in Sunnyside. And even at the end he is staying with Ellen in—is it in New Orleans?

Percy: No, he's over at a place like this, a place like Covington. I hadn't thought about it, but I guess there is a parallel there so that he's a little like Candide who was cultivating his garden, a small garden, you know. He's not totally given up, but partially giving up the grandiose idea of reforming the world, reforming the fallen condition of man by his lapsometer—what he calls angelism-bestialism. He's now fairly well content to live with Ellen, I guess her name is, a lusty Presbyterian wife on the bayou down in the slave quarter, which I thought was a good place to be, and running his trotline. There's a fellow out here who has a trotline right across that stretch of bayou right there. He's had it here for fifteen years. He checks his trotline every afternoon and every morning. Maybe that gave me the idea. I thought it was nice for Tom, after all that crap about the lapsometer and curing angelism-bestialism, which, of course, is the disease of the twentieth century—he was right about that; he was just wrong about thinking he could cure it or isolate it and cure it, to isolate it and cure it by a device. But his instincts were good in finally being better off under the bluff in a little cottage in the slave quarter and catching a—he caught a—gaspergou, I think.

Jones: Yes. Do you remember the first time you ever saw your Uncle Will?

Percy: Sure. In fact, I described it.

Jones: Right, in the introduction to *Lanterns on the Levee*.

Percy: Yes, in that introduction. I remember that very distinctly. I don't know whether you want me to say the same thing I said in the foreword.

Jones: I was interested to get you to describe for the tape how you came to live in Greenville and how he came to offer that invitation.

Percy: My father had died in Birmingham in the summer of 1929. It was a death by suicide. My mother had nothing to do but to take us three boys, my two brothers and myself, to move back to Athens, Georgia, with her mother, my grandmother Phinizy. It was a big house on Milledge Avenue in Athens. Well, you know how kids are—they don't take that sort of thing too seriously. You don't think too much about it. It was very pleasant living there in Athens. Looking back on it now, it must have been extremely traumatic for my mother. I remember I went to Athens High School as a freshman. I think I was thirteen. I spent one school year there. Then my Uncle Will shows up, I think in the spring sometime. I remember him very distinctly. The first time I ever saw him was when he came into my grandmother's house. He was a very striking-look-ing man, as I described him in that foreword. He must have thought of this for some time, but it was his proposal that we come and live with him in Greenville. So, again, at thirteen it didn't seem unusual, you know, why not? It seemed like a good idea, so we did. I think we moved down before the school started in the fall of 1930 and we moved in with him. He had this huge house. His mother and father had died; as you point out, his father had died about a year earlier. You say Christmas Eve, '29, huh?

Jones: Yes.

Percy: So. And his mother had died and he had an empty house, and we all moved in with him.

Jones: Your mother too?
Percy: Yes. My mother, who was not well, died about two years later. She was in an automobile accident. That happened in 1932. The household consisted then of my uncle plus these three boys. I was fourteen by then, my brother Roy was twelve, and my younger brother was seven or eight. So there we were, three boys and a bachelor in this house in Greenville, which no longer exists, by the way.
Jones: Right. I've always found it hard to fathom that here was a globe-trotting bachelor, a sensitive poet, lawyer, and planter who had all these concerns. Why in the world, what kind of commitment did he feel strong enough to take on three young boys?
Percy: That's a good question. I'm not sure I can answer it.
Jones: Was he that concerned with his family to go wherever there was suffering in it?
Percy: I think he was drawn in two directions. On the one hand he was a poet. He was a great lover of foreign places, particularly Greece, the Mediterranean—Taormina, Sicily, was, I think, his favorite place—and the South Seas. In fact, when we first saw him he'd just gotten back from living in Bora Bora for six months. But on the other hand, he always had a very strong sense of commitment to his region. I think this had to do with the very complicated and strong bond with his father. He felt the sense of carrying on his father's commitment, which you spoke of earlier, to make one place a little better. In fact he had been very active in flood relief in 1927 under the Hoover Commission, so he knew what it was to contribute to a local community. And he had a very strong sense of family. He was very attached to my father, and his father was, too. I think maybe he had the notion of giving us the benefit of exposure to him and of a good education, of giving us advantages that maybe we wouldn't have had other-

11

wise. But there was always a sense of conflict. After all, it was a crushing responsibility for somebody like him to take on. I'm always amazed at the fact that he did it.

Jones: He ended up adopting you three, didn't he?

Percy: He adopted us, yes, after my mother died.

Jones: Tell me something about growing up in his house. Did he push on you any ideas of academic excellence, or was he a domineering parent?

Percy: No.

Jones: What type of household did he run?

Percy: It was a strange household. He was the standard stopover for anybody who was traveling around the South, you know, that wanted to make a tour of the South. His house was one of the standard stops. All sorts of people came by to visit or spend the night. Dave Cohn came to spend a weekend and stayed a year. I don't know whether you know Dave Cohn's work?

Jones: *God Shakes Creation.*

Percy: Yes. And there were psychiatrists like Hortense Powdermaker and Harry Stack Sullivan. He came for three weeks and sat in the kitchen and drank vodka martinis. He was supposed to be studying the race problem. He thought it was a good place to go, and he probably was correct.

Jones: Talking to the cook.

Percy: Yes. Sure. And nobody had ever heard of vodka martinis in 1939 or '40. Carl Sandburg and the Benets, poets, and all sorts of people like that. Who was the fellow who did *A Southerner Discovers the South*—from Raleigh, you know? [Jonathan Daniels]

Jones: Roark Bradford?

Percy: No, but Roark and Dave Cohn came up. Raleigh—a newspaper man. So we were exposed to all manner of folk like that, and his own friends around Greenville were all sorts and classes of whites and blacks. It was an unusual sort of experience to grow up in a household like that. I guess the most important thing, you mentioned education, the most important

12

thing was he thought it was okay for us to go to Greenville High School, and it was.

Jones: You were the only one of you three to graduate from there, weren't you?

Percy: Right. That was because my brother had difficulty with Latin, so he got shipped off to Episcopal High School.

Jones: Didn't Will go to Episcopal High School?

Percy: He went to Sewanee.

Jones: Did he try to encourage you to go?

Percy: No, he thought it was a good idea, and it was, to go to Greenville High School, which is a good school. I was always glad I did. That's where I met Shelby [Foote]. And just yesterday my friend Charles Bell came by here. I don't know whether you've heard of him.

Jones: The poet?

Percy: The poet, yes. Charles was in my same class in high school—we were talking about that—and Shelby was in the class behind us. So I wouldn't have met Charles Bell or Shelby if I'd gone to Episcopal High School.

Jones: I know you've said that your Uncle Will made available to you a vocation, and, I believe you say, a second self that, for better or worse, wouldn't have otherwise been open to you. How would you say he influenced you in terms of your studying medicine and later turning to writing?

Percy: He didn't, as far as medicine. He put no pressure at all on me as far as choosing the law or any education. I think what happened was I felt obliged to go into a profession. I didn't want to go into law. It's like a hangover from the old Southern tradition of "what do you do?" Maybe it goes back to the English or the Europeans. Certain vocations are open to you, you know. What is it? Law, medicine, army, and priesthood. I got it down to medicine, which is a hell of a bad reason for going into medicine. No, he had nothing to do with that. That's an interesting question. I wonder what would have happened if I had said to him I wanted to be a writer, if I'd said, "I think I'll just take off two or three years and just travel around." I wonder what he would have said. Of course nowadays it's much more common for a young man to do exactly what he likes and to get away with it, which is good. The pressure didn't come from him; it came from me thinking what I was supposed to do, what one was expected to do, or maybe what he expected me to do. These things get internalized, you know. It's not what your parents actually want you or tell you to do; it's what you think you're supposed to do. How do you account for the fact that Greenville in that ten or fifteen years produced so many writers, you know, people interested in writing and poetry and music? Most people think, and I think Shelby would agree, that it was Uncle Will. He had this extraordinary capacity for communicating enthusiasm for beauty. He had this great love which I'd never seen before, which was unusual and is even now to see somebody who actually gets a high delight, great joy out of listening to music. I'd never seen somebody put on a stack of records of Beethoven's Ninth Symphony or Brahms' First Symphony—in those days they came in seventy-eight shellacs; you put a whole stack of them on his big Capehart, and then they'd drop down, you know—and listen to that with great pleasure. I didn't know what he was up to, you know; it was a phenomenon, like "What is that all about?" The first time I heard it, I couldn't make head or tail of it. He would just say, "Well, just listen to it." I can remember experiencing the breakthrough. After you listen to it, all of a sudden it's like a door opening; all of a sudden you are aware of what's going on. The same thing went for music, poetry, Shakespeare. Those were his big ones. Reading aloud, he could communicate that there was something

here, which is something that you rarely get in school
from a teacher. But he had this extraordinary capacity
for excitement. It was unique in my experience, seeing
somebody truly excited and experiencing real pleasure
at reading Shakespeare or listening to Brahms or Edna
St. Vincent Millay. Well, she was about as modern as
he got. He didn't get much past the end of the
nineteenth century. He ended mostly with Matthew
Arnold. I don't think he had much use for—I can't
remember any modern poets he liked. Millay—as I recall he liked some things of hers. To answer your question, that was the gift he gave me. He gave me the
excitement of reading. Writing? No, I don't think that
ever crossed his mind or mine that I could take up
writing. On the contrary, I remember one time we had
a poetry contest at Greenville High School, and he,
poor man, got suckered into being the judge. I won the
contest, even though the entries were anonymous and
numbered, and he said, "Well, I'm sorry you won, but
you needn't be happy about it because it was the worst
bunch of poems I've ever had occasion to judge." That
was the end of my poetry writing. They were very bad.
I think Shelby was in that same contest.
Jones: He has said, "Walker and I had some poetry in
the Greenville High School *Pica*, and you can go back
in the files and find them, I'm afraid."
Percy: Yes, I was writing a poem the first time I saw
Shelby. It was in the study hall. I don't know whether
he told you this or not. I wrote a poem and had it
typed, and he was sitting next to me and said, "What
are you doing?" I said, "I'm writing a poem," and he
looked at it and read it. It wasn't a very good poem. It
had never crossed his mind to write anything either. So
shortly after that he began to write some poetry which
was actually, although he would deny it, no better than
mine, which is to say they were terrible. So, yes, we
wrote some poetry in high school.

15

Jones: Do you think your poetry writing was part of an effort to show something to your uncle, to get closer to him?

Percy: You know, I have no idea, because I didn't show it to him. Maybe I thought since he was a poet and I had got some notion of what he liked in poetry that it might be fun to do. I never showed it to him. It was something to do.

Jones: At that age in high school, were you reading modern fiction or poetry?

Percy: Not really. I was more interested in science. I wasn't thinking about literature. In high school the only literary experience I can remember offhand was reading *Gone With the Wind*. When did that come out? It must have been the early '30s.

Jones: Thirty-six, same year as *Absalom, Absalom!*

Percy: I remember *Gone With the Wind* and *The Brothers Karamazov*, which is a pretty strange pair when you come to think of it; one of them a really great novel and the other, you know, a very good pop novel. I can remember the great reading experience of beginning to read *Gone With the Wind* and taking it to my grandmother's house and sitting on the front porch—we went back to visit her—sitting on her front porch in Athens and reading the whole thing in about three or four days, and doing the same thing with *The Brothers Karamazov* in Greenville. Also, my uncle put me onto a book he liked a lot called *Jean Christophe*, Romain Rolland. That was a very exciting experience. As the kids say, "I really dug that. I got on to that." How I got on to Dostoyevsky I don't know because he was not an admirer of Dostoyevsky.

Jones: He wasn't?

Percy: Not that I recall, no. I got that from Shelby. Shelby was always a very precocious reader, a good reader. Shelby might have got on to him before I did.

Jones: You two were close all the way through college?

Percy: Yes.

Jones: This is a question that I've asked everyone in
this project. I understand that Greenville had only one
farce of a lynching, one bad lynching . . .

Percy: It did?

Jones: They lynched the wrong man.

Percy: Hm.

Jones: And that the Klan never gained control of the
local politics and that Hodding Carter could come
there and write freely his type of journalism. And I
have learned in doing this civil rights project that I told
you about that among those people Greenville was
known as the country club of the Delta, less lethal.

Percy: Less dangerous, yes.

Jones: . . . that all of this is directly attributable to
the atmosphere that Will and the Senator created in
Greenville. Do you think it's as simple as that, or do
you know of any other factors?

Percy: I've wondered about that. I don't think that
you can trace it back to just one or two people. It must
have been that there was some sort of a humane tradition there. I think there must have been other people
involved. They were the ones I happen to know about.
Of course it was extremely important that my uncle and
Dave Cohn were instrumental in getting Hodding Carter up there in the '30s and put him in business with
the newspaper—and the roles that my brother Roy and
his son played. I think that was extraordinarily important. I feel very strongly that a newspaper sets the
whole political climate of a place. And Hodding went
through some very tough times; he had a hard time. It
wasn't as easy as some people like to imagine. He suf-
fered several indignities of having garbage dumped on
his lawn and such like. So yes, I know my uncle was
very important and Uncle LeRoy. It was certainly important for Uncle Will to have gotten Hodding Carter
there. I hope that the cycle hasn't come to an end,

because I understand that the Carters have sold the paper to a southern California newspaper chain, which doesn't sound so good. I'll have to wait and see. It would be very sad for that paper, that tradition to come to an end and Greenville to lose its uniqueness, because the whole time I was there and knew anything about it, it was not like other Mississippi towns. To answer your question, I would have to give these names: Uncle LeRoy, Uncle Will, my brother LeRoy, his son Billy, the Carters.

Jones: Can you think of any other factors that you remember growing up there that might have contributed to its liberalism?

Percy: Hm. I'm not really sure how liberal it was. All I can think of is that my uncle's house was open to all sorts of people, black and white. Langston Hughes came there once and spent the night. That was funny because my uncle, being the idealist and liberal that he was, introduced him at a meeting by saying, "Now here's a man who's black and a poet and who has risen above the issues of race and ideologies involved in being a black activist and who's now become a poet." Whereupon Langston Hughes got up and read the most ideologically aggressive poetry you can imagine. I think my Uncle Will expected a little too much for a black poet in the 1930s to have risen above the matters of race. For me it was my uncle, Will Percy, and the Carters, the paper, who were the main influences. My uncle was absolutely fearless. He wasn't afraid of anybody. That and the newspaper being very influential among people of character, plus the fact that the Carter newspaper bought out the other newspaper and became the only newspaper, was a very powerful influence on the way Greenville was.

Jones: I wanted to pick up on something that you said. You said your uncle wasn't scared of anybody. You know, nowadays when people bring up the name

Will Percy, especially young history professors and
such, he seems to have a Blanche DuBois reputation. I
heard James Silver giving a talk on civil rights down at
Millsaps [College] saying that he and Dave Cohn were
investigating the possibilities of integrated dinners as
early as the late 1930s, "while," quote, "while Dave's
friend Will Percy bemoaned the passing of the days
when blacks displayed good manners." I've always
thought that was unfair because he was something else
again in his day.

Percy: Yes. He addressed himself to that whole issue
in *Lanterns on the Levee*, and I talked about my feelings
about it in the foreword to it. There again we're a
victim of our own times. It's easy to look back now and
say that he was a segregationist or paternalistic, and
maybe in a sense that's true. It was also true that in his
day he was regarded as a liberal, a dangerous liberal, by
his friends and contemporaries in Greenville. It's easy
for somebody like Silver, who is a comfortable academic
liberal, to denigrate what Will Percy did in the 1920s
and '30s. All I know is that he repeatedly got himself
in trouble with the sheriff's department, with the
police, for attacking them in public for police brutality.
I can remember black people coming to the house
who'd been imprisoned and beaten up, and he would
take them in and defend them and attack the sheriff's
office or the chief of police, in public, and was branded
as a "niggcr lovcr" and such. It's very easy to look back
and criticize from our comfortable liberal perspective
now. It's very easy to be a liberal in Mississippi and
Louisiana these days; in fact it's downright chic. It
wasn't then!

Jones: I know his house was kind of a boarding house
for the passing literary figures, but can you tell me
something about his friends in Greenville? Who was he
close to there?

Percy: I'm trying to think who his close friends were:

Ada and Charlie Williams, two old family friends; the
Shields brothers, Tommy and Arnold Shields; Rufus
Mock and his wife. It was not a particular class. His
friends were not limited to, quote, "the upper classes."
He had friends on all levels, and black friends. I remember one black guy who was more or less off the
street. He'd walk up and down the street at night and
talk to people. One black guy came in one Sunday and
played the blues on the harmonica for several hours.
But who were his best friends? My brother Roy would
remember those people better than I. I don't know if
you asked him the same question. He's been there all
his life and I haven't been there since 1945.

Jones: When did you leave Greenville for good?

Percy: After he died in 1942. I only came back to visit
my brother, so I guess it was '42. After that I was
either in medical school or—I contracted tuberculosis
working as an intern at Bellevue Hospital doing au-
topsies on TB deaths. For two years I was, quote, "taking the cure," as we said, at Saranac Lake in New York,
and also working as a doctor up there, which was the
best thing that ever happened to me because it gave me
a chance to quit medicine. I had a respectable excuse.
For two years I could read anything. I read for two
years.

Jones: Yes.

Percy: After my scientific education I had time to
read.

Jones: Yes, I want to talk about that some more, but
let me ask you a couple more questions about your
Uncle Will.

Percy: Yes.

Jones: Were you at home when he died, or were you
taking the cure?

Percy: No, I was interning. I was at Bellevue.

Jones: Did you come home?

Percy: Yes. I came home twice; once when he got very

sick, I went back to Bellevue, and when he died, my
brother called me. He died suddenly. I think he died in
April of '42.

Jones: January, I believe.

Percy: Well, that could be. I was with him when he
first got sick. *Lanterns on the Levee* had just come out,
and he was enjoying the reviews. We were at Sewanee.
I went to Sewanee with him and his driver David,
David Scott—I think it was David. It was in the summer. *Lanterns on the Levee* must have come out in May or
June of '41. It's funny; it came out the same month,
the same year, and from the same publishing house as
The Mind of the South.

Jones: W. J. Cash.

Percy: It's strange. There couldn't be two more different books about the South, and yet both are very valuable in their way. We were staying at Brinkwood, his
summer place at Sewanee. He was enjoying himself
very much because he loved to get letters, fan mail, and
he was writing responses. One of his close friends was
Charlotte Gailor; in fact, she was one of the people he
dedicated the book to—it's to Ada, Charlotte and Tom,
and to me, Roy, and Phin. We went to see Charlotte
Gailor, who was the daughter of the Bishop Gailor
there at Sewanee, and there were some students visiting
there too. They were having a meeting, three or four
students. He was talking, and all of a sudden what he
said didn't make any sense. I had just finished medical
school, so I had sense enough to know what had happened. It was an aphasic response, and probably he'd
had a small stroke in the area of the speech zone, of all
places to hit him, because he was very good, very articulate with language. He loved to talk to young people. He could talk very well. All of a sudden for this to
happen and for him not to be able to say what he
wanted to say; he was very much aware of it. He was
aware of what was going on and what was happening

and the fact that he was aphasic and couldn't make himself known, so he grabbed me by the arm and said in effect, "Let's get out of here." I knew what had happened, so I took him home. I didn't have as much as a blood pressure apparatus with me. I called old Dr. Kirby-Smith the next day, from the old Kirby-Smith family at Sewanee, and he came out and took his blood pressure. It was some ungodly reading like 280 over 150 or something like that. It was malignant hypertension. He recovered from that particular episode. He regained his speech. I took him to Johns Hopkins immediately. Another great friend and also a distant relative was Janet Longcope—Janet Dana who married Warfield Longcope who was head of the medical division at Johns Hopkins. That was the best place I could think of. I took him up there and stayed with him for about a week or so. They did all the diagnostic tests and diagnosed him as having malignant hypertension. In those days there was not much you could do about it. Now you can treat it. There were very few drugs you could give. There wasn't too much, Longcope didn't offer too much, so I brought him back to Greenville. He got a little better. He never regained his strength really. I remember being there for the Christmas holidays. My internship didn't begin until January, so I was home for the month of December. He was feeling better, was up and around and could talk. I can remember him coming out on Sunday afternoon, December 7, 1941. Of course, you know what that was.

Jones: Pearl Harbor.

Percy: Everybody who's old enough can remember exactly where they were at that moment. I do. We were in the sun parlor of the old house and Uncle Will came out at two o'clock in the afternoon. He loved Japanese kimonos. He had a black Japanese kimono on. He kept all of his stuff in his sleeve. He came out in a big hurry and said, "The Japanese have attacked the fleet at Pearl

Harbor." He was delighted, because he'd wanted the
United States to enter the war long before. For him this
was, in a sense, good news. It meant we were in the
war. He would've gone to war six months before that.
In fact he tried to.

Jones: Yes, Roy told me that. Do you need to stop?

Percy: I want you to meet my wife. (Whistles)

Jones: I'd like that.

Mrs. Percy: Hi.

Jones: Hi. (Tape off while introductions being made;
pick up with conversation among Jones, Dr. Percy, and
his wife Bunt)

Percy: I left to pick her [Mrs. Percy] up at three
o'clock in the afternoon, and I said, "The war has
started," and she said, "What war?" I said, "Like the
world war." I don't think you took it in. So we went
out to the levee with a .22 and shot at things, and
somebody stole your purse. Everybody remembers
where they were on Sunday afternoon, December 7, just
as you probably remember where you were when Kennedy got shot.

Jones: Yes. I wanted to ask you something about Kennedy's assassination. I read where you said that the
assassination cost you a year's work on *The Last Gentleman*.

Percy: It was a long time. I don't know how long it
was.

Jones: Did you know about Phinizy's connection with
John Kennedy?

Percy: Yes. Sure.

Jones: They were commanders in the Navy together or
something?

Percy: No, they were lieutenants on the PT boats at
Guadalcanal in 1942. Things were very tough. In fact
my brother, as he will tell you—or maybe he won't, I
don't know whether he wants to talk about it or not—
he was in the same squadron as Kennedy and he was in

the boat behind Kennedy when Kennedy got rammed by that Japanese destroyer. He'll tell you the story if he wants to. You can ask him about it.

Jones: Yes, I will. To return one last time: your Uncle Will did contract aphasia right toward the end of his life?

Percy: I don't know, I guess he did. I don't remember. I remember that particular attack. I know Miss Charlotte Gailor. . .

Mrs. Percy: He had exactly the same thing my mother had, and it followed about the same pattern.

Percy: That's true, and she was about the same age.

Mrs. Percy: Right, they were exactly the same age and they were both dead within six months.

Percy: Well, he was born in '88 [actually he was born May 14, 1885] and died in '42; that would make him fifty-four, wouldn't it? He had the arteries of a man eighty years old.

Jones: What would be the cause of that?

Percy: Well, they call it malignant hypertension. That's not a diagnosis, it's a description. They still don't know the cause of that.

Mrs. Percy: Some people just have terrific high blood pressure that never comes down.

Percy: Except that now they can treat it.

Mrs. Percy: I'm not so sure they can treat it.

Percy: Well, they can treat a good deal of it.

Mrs. Percy: What did they use to treat Mr. Will with, do you remember? I don't remember what they used to treat my mother. They were giving massive doses of garlic.

Jones: Garlic?

Mrs. Percy: Yes, and then something else.

Percy: Tell John what you thought of Uncle Will the first time you saw him.

Mrs. Percy: Oh, I was terrified of him.

Jones: Are you from Greenville?

Mrs. Percy: Yes. I was a technician and the doctor came by—I was dating Walker and Mr. Will knew that I was, I'm pretty sure, because I got teased a lot. Huger Jervey was a great friend of his. Have you come across Huger Jervey's name at all?

Jones: I know Gervis Lusk.

Mrs. Percy: No. Huger Jervey was a great friend of Mr. Will's. He was—I don't know whether he was head of the law school at Columbia, but he would come down and visit for long periods of time. He was a great tease, and when Walker would come to see me, they would say, "Bye baby bunting, Daddy's gone a-hunting." My name was Bunt. I knew him because Walker told me these little funny stories and I was just terrified to go over there. The doctor came in and said, "We have to make a house call." That just meant you went on a house call to take a blood sample. When I got in the car and found out where I was going, I was even more petrified. I remember walking in the house and right through the study and then, I think there was a step-up to his bedroom. He had on a green Japanese coat, I guess you would call it, with the big sleeves. He was very impressive looking.

Jones: Was he?

Mrs. Percy: Yes, very impressive. In fact, my hand was shaking when I got down to him. You remember that bedroom off from where he was sick?

Percy: Yes.

Mrs. Percy: I had to stick his finger in there and my hand was shaking.

Percy: Why were you so afraid of him?

Mrs. Percy: I think because you had told me about Huger teasing you. Do you remember? He doesn't know anything about Huger, who was a great friend of his.

Percy: Oh, that's another very good friend of his. You had asked me about friends from Greenville. This is

Huger Jervey, his great friend from Sewanee, professor at Columbia University whom I lived with a year or so after I moved to New York.

Mrs. Percy: And he would come and stay for long periods of time.

Percy: Yes.

Mrs. Percy: I think he was probably one of Mr. Will's best friends.

Percy: Yes, he was. The others were, let's see . . .

Mrs. Percy: Then we took him on after that. He came and spent time at Sewanee with us.

Percy: One of the good friends that we knew about was Gerstle Mack. Gerstle Mack is still living, incidentally. That reminds me, I got a Christmas card from him. We'll have to call him up.

Jones: Tell me for the tape how you two happened to meet.

Mrs. Percy: Same way I met Mr. Will, sticking his finger.

Percy: Did you stick my finger?

Mrs. Percy: Yes.

Percy: I wonder what I was doing. Was I sick?

Mrs. Percy: Oh, yes, you were sick.

Jones: This was when you were in med school or after?

Percy: No, I don't think so.

Mrs. Percy: This was before he went to med school.

Percy: This was . . .

Mrs. Percy: No, you came over to the clinic, and . . . some way you were at the clinic.

Percy: No, no. I was getting a job. I had six months between the end of medical school and the beginning of internship in 1941, so I thought it would be nice to go back to my uncle's house because he was sick, for one thing, and get a job at the local clinic, and I did. She was working at the clinic. She was a medical technologist at the Gamble Clinic in Greenville.

Mrs. Percy: Mr. Will told Walker he could buy himself a car, and guess what Walker bought. You're not

going to believe it: a green Packard convertible. He
went from a nothing car, what was it? A little old
Ford?

Percy: Yes.

Mrs. Percy: To a Packard, which he kept only three
months, I think, before he got sick.

Percy: True, true.

Jones: This was right after you got out of med school?

Percy: I guess so, yes.

Jones: And this was your graduation present.

Percy: He was rewarding me, I guess.

Mrs. Percy: That was after med school. But didn't I
meet you right after North Carolina before you went to
med school?

Percy: I don't think so—after medical school.

Jones: I think this is interesting. I'm glad you all
agree to talk about it on the tape. I don't think I've
ever heard that story.

Mrs. Percy: Well, I think I knew Walker for about
seven years before we married. I'm going backward. I
was about eighteen when I met you, and I was twenty-
six when we married.

Percy: Hm. I thought it was the fall of '41 when I met
you, when I was working at the clinic. When I was out
in Sante Fe in 1945, that would be four years later. . . .
We got married in '46, didn't we?

Mrs. Percy: Yes. I thought it was more than that.

Jones: You and Shelby went out to Sante Fe, didn't
you?

Percy: Yes.

Jones: This was right after he got discharged.

Percy: Yes, I believe it was. This was after Bilbo's last
campaign. He did a speech in Leland at which Hodding
Carter accused him of saying something like . . . somebody accused him of being anti-Semitic.

Jones: When he said, "I like every damn Jew from
Jesus Christ on down."

Mrs. Percy: Yes, I heard that.

Percy: Yes, he was saying that, and I was there. Hodding Carter wanted me to sign a deposition that he had in fact said that. I signed it. I didn't live anywhere. I was visiting my brother and I got to the point where I decided to move on. I said, "Shelby, why don't we go out to Santa Fe?" So we left and went to Sante Fe. I lived on a ranch for about two or three months.

Jones: Why Santa Fe?

Percy: Always liked it, always liked it. Shelby stayed for a couple of weeks.

Mrs. Percy: Well, you still like the idea of the mountains and all that. We thought about living there.

Percy: It's beautiful, clear, high country.

Jones: And then you came back and where did you go?

Percy: I came back and went to New Orleans. She was working for a doctor in New Orleans. We married in '46, I guess. See, I was a free agent. I was at loose ends, didn't know what I wanted to do. I was out of medical school, and I don't think I've ever considered going back into medicine. I don't know whether I was thinking of being a writer by then, or a bum, or what.

Mrs. Percy: Well, you got a bad x-ray right after we got married.

Percy: So I had to take it easy.

Mrs. Percy: You started intensive reading, and that's when you were wanting to write on things you really wanted to say, but you decided nobody would read it. That's how you got into novels. You wrote that first article.

Percy: I don't remember when it was. I do remember we spent the first winter at Sewanee in Uncle Will's place where I had been a few years before with him, you see, when he first got sick. So I guess I did have to go take the cure again up there.

Mrs. Percy: You were in bed most of the time up there.

Percy: After a year there we decided we didn't want to

live there. I don't know how we hit on New Orleans. How did we hit on New Orleans? I've forgotten. I didn't want to live in Greenville, didn't want to go back there, and it never crossed my mind to go back to a place like Birmingham or Athens or Memphis; but New Orleans, you know, I always liked the idea. So we lived in New Orleans another winter.

Mrs. Percy: That was kind of an interesting story. We came down to look for a place to stay and we were just going through ads in the paper when we came to a house on Calhoun Street. It belonged to Julius Friend, who happened to know Mr. Will.

Percy: One of the many who'd visited the house, with Roark Bradford.

Mrs. Percy: We had no idea who owned the house. We dropped in on them and of course they rented us the house, left us their maid, their furniture, their silverware.

Percy: Yes, that was a case of Jungian synchronicity. It turned out to be Julius Friend who was a friend of Uncle Will's, and the house was built by old man McDowell who had the place next to Brinkwood at Sewanee. It was really strange.

Mrs. Percy: I'm not sure I can believe that story, because how did he ever get away from the mountains?

Percy: Well, I think he lived in New Orleans before that.

Mrs. Percy: He did? That story was told.

Percy: It's absolutely true.

Jones: Tell me this, Dr. Percy; when did writing become an option for you? Were you thinking about writing first and then moved into medicine and then from your experience with tuberculosis move back into writing?

Percy: Well, I don't know. I enjoyed writing even back at Greenville High School for the local paper, *The Pica*, and later writing for the college paper. But, as I

29

say, it never crossed my mind to go into it profession-
ally, except that I did like to do it. When did I start
seriously? I don't know. Let's see. I think somewhere in
the '50s, I read some things that excited me.

Mrs. Percy: Susanne Langer's book?

Percy: Susanne Langer's book, yes. It was a very pro-
vocative book. I agreed with it in some things and
disagreed with it in other things, so I wrote a review of
it. I sent it off to a journal, *Thought Quarterly*, and it
was published. I liked that idea.

Mrs. Percy: Yes, he liked that.

Percy: Even though I didn't get paid. They sent me
back fifty reprints. I said, "This is for me," you know.
Fortunately, I had enough money that my uncle had
left me that I could afford to do that. I can't imagine
how anybody starts writing. I didn't support myself for
years. If you're not an academic or you're not a pop
writer, I don't know how you do it. I went from that to
writing a few occasional pieces for *Commonweal*, a liberal
Catholic newspaper, journal, weekly. I did several
pieces for them and got paid like twenty-five dollars. I
liked that too. Somewhere along there I began to write
a novel.

Mrs. Percy: You wrote for *Philosophy and Phenomenological Research* and *Psychiatry*.

Percy: I wrote some articles, yes. But I can't remember when I made up my mind that "maybe I can make a
living at this," or "maybe I could make a career of it." I
don't remember when that happened.

Mrs. Percy: I remember when your book got accepted.

Percy: Well, yes.

Jones: *The Moviegoer?*

Percy: Yes.

Jones: What do you remember of that?

Mrs. Percy: I was outside laying a brick patio. I think
I was mad at him about something. If I was working
that hard, I must have been. He came to the window
and hollered out, and I forgot I was supposed to be mad

at him then. He said, "It's been accepted." We were both excited.

Jones: I want to ask you something else. Talking about Shelby again: I've always been surprised at the way his early fiction has been kind of glossed-over by critics. *Follow Me Down* is a fine novel. But I suppose to read even the first few pages of his Civil War trilogy is to think that here's a guy who has found his great subject.

Percy: Yes.

Jones: What do you think of his fiction and his work?

Percy: Well, I think his fiction does not now receive its just criticism. I agree with you; *Follow Me Down*, *Love in a Dry Season* and *Shiloh*, maybe particularly *Shiloh*, I think are remarkable. They have been re-printed, they're back in print. It is true that he took off twenty years to write that mammoth Civil War thing, which I think is an extraordinary thing to do, requiring no end of persistence, and knowing exactly what he was doing and doing it very well. I think it's the best history of its kind. It was such a happy marriage of his fictional art and his first-class history; he's a good historian. It was such a happy conjunction of these two faculties. It lasted so long that it might have made it difficult for him to get back into writing fiction. I thought the novel he wrote afterwards has been under-valued. The critics didn't really take to it very well— *September September*. I liked it better than most of the critics. As you know, he's got a major work afoot now. I don't know whether he's started or not. He's been thinking about it for years. It's a very large novel.

Jones: Called *Two Gates to the City?*

Percy: Yes.

Jones: I think his achievement in that Civil War trilogy is just astounding; sentence after sentence, page after page for three massive volumes, so skillfully written. It's just good history.

Percy: Yes.

Jones: You have a rare past for a Southern novelist and you've broken new ground in Southern literature. Do you think it is more a product of your unique background in medicine and your readings in existentialist philosophy and your Catholicism, or do you think you take this new direction because the old tradition is dead?

Percy: Well, I think it's probably all of those, a conjunction of circumstances. One is the scientific background, which is a strange background for a novelist, but valuable, I think. I think it leads both to an appreciation of scientific truth and elegance on the one hand, and on the other how the scientific method and the use of technology estranges a person: how somebody who follows the scientific method and comes to its logical conclusion can end up as a sort of an outsider, to be outside his own method. That's a problem that Binx Bolling deals with in *The Moviegoer*. You got that, the scientific background. The exposure to Will Percy, who was a very powerful influence—this man, what he stood for. Also, for me to break through into philosophy, most importantly the modern French existentialists going back to the Russian novelists, Dostoyevsky, all the way back to Thomas Aquinas and Augustine, and finally my conversion to the Catholic Church. Living here in Covington is kind of between the Catholic South and the Protestant Bible Belt. I've always enjoyed the conflict of cultures: the scientific on the one hand, humanistic on the other; the Catholic South and the Protestant North; Will Percy's traditional Southern culture and Binx Bolling's alienation, being outside of it. Binx Bolling, you see, has straddled both of them. On the other hand he comes from the typical Gulf Coast, Louisiana Catholic, middle-class Catholic background. It's a dialectical thing, I guess. It's the interaction between these two cultures, three cultures. That's what makes a novel work when it works. It's how these influences interact and how they are resolved, or not resolved.

Jones: Can you tell me a little of what went into your decision not to practice medicine? Was it an intellectual thing, or could you simply not do it physically?

Percy: I could have done it physically. I was never'that sick. In fact, I didn't have any symptoms. I had what was called a minimal lesion. It was picked up on a routine x-ray. I didn't have any cough or fever or any of that. Sure, I could have gone back into medicine. I think that period of reading and the idea of being onto something, of reading something, reading modern philosophers and thinking, "This man might be onto something," or "This woman, Susanne Langer, was onto something and she lost it, she dropped it, she fumbled the ball." I got excited by it, the philosophy of language, the philosophy of, quote, "existentialism," what was called then existentialism, in a way that medicine never excited me. I think that there may be a kind of a—I don't know what they call it—a hope or a conceit or a conviction, or the idea that, well, if she missed it maybe I can pick it up. There was something here. There was something there to be found. There was something worth looking for. That was valuable. I think the best I could have done in medicine would have been maybe in psychiatry. I was thinking of doing that. But I was lucky because I wouldn't have had the—I didn't have nerve enough to set off to become a writer from the beginning. I was lucky to have gone through medicine and gone through a place like Bellevue Hospital, and that old-fashioned sanatorium like Thomas Mann's *Magic Mountain*. I think I was better off doing that than doing, say, what a—what would one do to become a writer? People always ask me that. "What do you do to become a writer?" I don't know. I guess I would have majored in English some place, North Carolina, then what, taken a Ph.D. in English, then what?

Jones: Some writers say that absolutely the worst thing that could happen to you as a writer is to be on a college campus.

Percy: Yes, not too much good comes off college campuses, not in the way of writing, which is not to put down college campuses, because I taught a couple of times. I don't see how anybody could teach and write at the same time. It's hard work.

Jones: Will says in *Lanterns on the Levee* that it taps the same reservoir.

Percy: I think it does. At least if you're conscientious it does.

Jones: I wanted to ask you how you came to decide on the novel as the way to express your philosophical concerns?

Percy: Well, three ways. One was that I soon discovered that nobody read philosophical articles, not even academics, especially when not written by an academic. Maybe academicians read each other, I don't know, but they didn't read mine. I don't think I ever got a letter from anybody who'd read one of those articles in a philosophical journal and said anything about it. One reason was there was no audience. It was like dropping a message into a void—no response. The other was that there was no money. The third thing was about that time I discovered the French facility for combining philosophy and art, or the novel or the play, which the French do very well. It's done often by people in different professions: in the profession of diplomacy or government, people like Claudel, Mauriac. I was excited by what Marcel and Sartre and Camus had done by having very strong ideas about the nature of things, the nature of man, and transmuting this into fictional form without somehow falling victim to pedantry or ideology, although Sartre ended up doing exactly that. I saw that it was possible to be excited by ideas, even philosophy, and not only to combine that with the novel, but to use it in the novel, to actually put it to good use, which the French had been doing and the Americans had not been doing too well, or even trying to do. The American novelist traditionally had been thought of as an adventurer in the concrete, particularly in the South—somebody who traffics in lore and history and stories and conversations and family sagas and so forth in the good old Faulkner-Welty tradition. It had not been a discovery of American literature to do what the French had done. Of course in this country you had the novelists over here and the artists here and the musicians and composers here and the businessmen here and the professors here and the philosophers over here. So it was quite a revelation to me to see somebody like Sartre, even though in the end I disagreed with him. Maybe one of the most influential novels I ever read was *Nausea.* That was a real revelation. It's funny how something can be that important and influence you that much and be that valuable to you, and yet you can diametrically disagree with it. It has usually worked with me that way. I may be mostly indebted to people with whom I have the deepest disagreements. They are the ones I owe the most to.

Jones: Right. I've read where you said, "You can be sure I didn't learn to write sitting on the front porch listening to old folks tell stories."

Percy: That's correct. That's right.

Jones: But there again I know that when you read Walker Percy, and his philosophical concerns are very valuable, original, and unique, what you are admiring of and what makes his work such sheer joy is his prose style.

Percy: Right.

Jones: I know the existentialists influenced you most

in terms of the construction of your ideology, but who
influenced your narrative style most?

Percy: Narrative style?

Jones: Yes, your prose style.

Percy: I think Dostoyevsky, Camus, and Sartre. Dostoyevsky in his idea of people obsessed with—these
characters who're obsessed with some idea or something, or find themselves in a certain situation, a terrible predicament, and behave accordingly. Camus for
the style, the sparseness, the laconic brevity, and precision of his sentences. Sartre for catching on to the value
of being a twentieth century outsider, man who is outside of it, and Sartre being able to use this and to see
the value of it. Psychiatrically it would be considered as
a pathology, a symptom. Literarily I saw that the great
value of what Sartre had done was to take the outsider
and use his very outsideness as a way of seeing things in
a different way. Who else? Well, from the Americans
I'd have to say Mark Twain.

Jones: I was going to ask you about Twain.

Percy: Yes. Mark Twain and Hemingway, and I guess
Faulkner, although I was scared to death of writing like
Faulkner. That's curious, though. Even though I've
gone out of my way to avoid Faulkner, in spite of
my—because of my—admiration, nevertheless, I find
myself thinking, "Oh God, that sounds like him," you
know, when I write it. Faulkner is at once the blessing
and curse of all Southern novelists, maybe all novelists.

Jones: Because he so delineated the style?

Percy: Well, he's so good, and he's so overwhelming,
so big, and also so seductive, not necessarily in the
right kind of way. His very faults are seductive. That
involuted syntax is seductive, and not necessarily good
either. You find yourself falling victim to it—that is,
using it in a lazy kind of way, using it as an excuse not
to be precise the way that Camus would be precise. It's
so damn easy to fall victim to that.

Jones: And it probably makes for the worst type of literature if done badly.

Percy: That's right.

Jones: I was going to ask you about Mark Twain because it has always seemed to me that there was some connection between you two, especially as seen in the article you wrote for *Esquire* on bourbon.

Percy: Oh, yes?

Jones: I haven't laughed that hard at something I read since "The Literary Offenses of James Fenimore Cooper."

Percy: What was it that reminded you of Twain in that?

Jones: Well, just the humor.

Percy: Oh, just the approach?

Jones: Right. Kind of looking at it sideways.

Percy: I hadn't thought of that.

Jones: It was really funny.

Percy: Well, maybe, yes. That's true, Mark Twain's humor. I find humor very valuable.

Jones: You're very good at it.

Percy: Well, I discovered that the use of humor is not to be funny. I only found out later what Kierkegaard said, that humor is the most serious thing of all. Humor is not the opposite of being serious. He said that humor is the last stage, in going through the stages of life—he called them the aesthetic and the ethical and the religious—he said humor is the last stage before the religious. I thought that was an extraordinary statement. I just discovered that humor is a valuable technique in fiction. There's some strange quirk in the modern consciousness, the contemporary consciousness, so that one is more accessible, the reader is more accessible, and that there is some sort of communication that goes on between writer and reader which is facilitated through humor. I don't know exactly how that works except that it's just been given various names, like black humor—you know, humor used kind of perversely or sick or whatever. It does have a valuable function which I haven't quite identified.

Jones: Shelby Foote says that every page of great literature has at least some element of humor in it.

Percy: Yes.

Jones: So you steer clear of gin fizzes as you said in the *Esquire* article?

Percy: Oh, yes. Yes, that really happened to me, that gin fizz thing.

Jones: You and Dr. Tom More.

Percy: I guess. He had it too, didn't he?

Jones: Yes. You said it made your lip stick out like a shelf, like Mortimer Snerd.

Percy: True, true.

Jones: Oh, yes. Let me ask you this too, to kind of make a bow toward this other project that I'm doing on the civil rights movement. Early on in your career you expressed at least a sympathy with that movement and its objectives, but by the time of *Love in the Ruins* and *Lancelot* you had taken the sentiments of those movement people and kind of satirized them. Lancelot makes fun of his NAACP connections. Do you think that the movement got kind of misdirected toward the end?

Percy: No, I don't. I use that purely as a means of drawing the character of a particular person in a novel. The satire comes in view of a person who thinks he can find his own course in life through liberal causes. The NAACP was admirable, the civil rights movement was admirable, but it was also a way of avoiding one's self. One could give one's self the civil rights movement and escape one's self for the next ten years, both for the very serious, idealistic young, and for a man like Lancelot who was middle-aged, cynical, who nevertheless came off as a liberal of sorts who wanted to do the right thing, quote, "the right thing" about the interracial thing. Also, for him it was a little cynical. He was doing it maybe to irritate his neighbors. I guess that is

38

a legacy of the existentialist tradition. Marcel always talked about being wary of mass movements or causes. There's always a danger of taking up a cause, of being too much identified with a cause. Also the political thing is that the civil rights movement has won, in a sense. It has won as much as any political movement has won, so that the blacks, I think, have made their point to a degree, which is not to say, God knows, that there aren't still serious areas of injustice and brutality and racism. They've won to the extent that a young black man can do pretty much what he wants, or he's a lot closer to it than he was twenty or thirty years ago. Also there's a danger from a novelist's point of view of taking on a liberal cause. There's no greater danger to fiction, I think, than ideology. I can't think offhand of any good novel which has been animated by the desire to oppose segregation, either from the black point of view or from the white point of view. If you set out to write a novel and your main motivation is the abolition of segregation or racism, it's almost fatal. God knows how many bad novels have been written by both blacks and whites, passionate novels which indict racism. I can only think of one or two that survive, and they survive despite the passionate ideology. I'm thinking of *Native Son,* Wright's novel, and what's the other one?

Jones: Ralph Ellison's *Invisible Man?*

Percy: *The Invisible Man,* right.

Jones: Yes. It's a curious thing that Mississippi in ten years, or really from 1964 to 1970 when desegregation came about—I was in high school and it was largely peaceful—that Mississippi did a complete about-face in terms of history in an incredibly short period of time. I'm sure that you'll agree that that will have some effect on Mississippi being a spawning ground for writers.

Percy: Sure, right. And that's the good thing about at least the partial victory of the civil rights movement: that they won thanks to, mainly, to Lyndon Johnson of all people—Martin Luther King and the activists, and then Lyndon Johnson. The good thing about that is that now you can address the middle-class black reader, or you're beginning to be able to, and you no longer have to be bothered about, "Well, racism is bad, and there's no way I can write for you because you have to achieve the middle-class American success before—you have to know how much trouble we're in before I can talk to you." There's no way you can write in good conscience to a person who's deprived of the ordinary means of life, who doesn't have what everybody else has. The single greatest change that happened in this country in the last fifty years has been this extraordinary revolution that you're talking about in Mississippi: the rise of the black middle class. Now you have a generation of blacks who are in as much trouble as affluent whites, and God knows that is a lot of trouble!

Jones: They didn't know what they were getting in for.

Percy: That's right. Now they know!

Jones: So Mississippi is no longer the land of, as you put it, "good-looking and ferocious young bigots." That was in the article you wrote for *Harper's* called "Mississippi: The Fallen Paradise."

Percy: I remember writing it, but I've forgotten what I said.

Jones: It was in '65.

Percy: Yes.

Jones: You wrote about how the proud tradition of the Mississippians involved in Pickett's Charge was being prostituted by those students at Ole Miss in '62.

Percy: Yes.

Jones: Well, I've just got a couple more questions. The only review of your work that I've ever read that was less than all-praising was written by John Gardner in the *New York Times Book Review* about *Lancelot.*

Percy: Yes.

Jones: Gardner said that while you adumbrate—I learned that word from you—the woes of modern soci-

ety and, as you put it, the "malaise" in the modern world better than any other modern fiction writer, that you don't take us across the river, you don't show us the fruits of the search. Do you see that as your role?
Percy: No, that's not my role.
Jones: He said that art today, in his opinion, ought to "stop sniveling, go for the answers, or shut up."
Percy: Yes, that's true, he thinks that art should be edifying, and that's not bad—edifying in the best sense. It should be, in the best sense. But I would agree with Kierkegaard there; he would say that art functions at the aesthetic level. Let's face it. We're limited. The most we could hope to do as artists, and that's what a writer is or what he hopes to be, is to point out certain home truths. Faulkner said it too. He called it "the motions of the human heart"—to say how it is, how it is to be alive and how we find ourselves and what's there. Kierkegaard said himself—he said, "I am not an apostle." In the aesthetic phase you can talk about how it is on the island, see, how it is in a certain time and a certain place in a certain culture, even a Christian culture, but what you can't do is you can't speak with the authority of an apostle. That's what Kierkegaard would say. He said himself, "I do not have the authority to tell you that God came into history and that therefore you should believe in Him." Now that's not for me to say. That's not for the novelist to say. The novelist can say how it is for a man in a certain state whether he's Christian or non-Christian or whatever—sinful, always sinful. But Gardner, I think, is confusing the aesthetic and the religious stage, at least in my mind. Maybe he can do it, but I can't. That's why the main criticism of my novels is that they all end indecisively, which is very deliberate. They'd be in big trouble if they ended decisively.
Jones: Am I right in saying that the search that you discuss in all of your novels is the important thing, rather than what's at the end of it?

Percy: Well, that's open. That's an open question.

Jones: Only in *Lancelot* is the search clear, and there, I suppose, the search is for the unholy grail, to find the reality of his wife's sin.

Percy: Yes.

Jones: Would you care to comment on the nature of the search in your other novels?

Percy: Well.

Jones: I know that's a hard one.

Percy: Yes. I think if the novels have found any response it's because anybody who has any sense at all finds himself in this culture in a state of confusion; that is, as Guardini would say, we're living in the post-modern world. The world has ended in a sense. We're living in one of these times that hasn't been named yet. Looking back on history, we can talk about the fall of the Roman Empire and what happened after that: the Dark Ages, the Middle Ages, High Middle Ages, the Renaissance, Reformation and so forth; something has happened now and we are not into it far enough to know what it is. We're living at the end of modern times. The end of modern times will be the end of Christendom as we know it. No one has named this period yet. We don't know what it is. So I think the normal state for a man to find himself in is in a state of confusion, spiritual disorientation, drawn in a sense to Christendom, but also repelled by the cultural nature of Christendom. To answer your question, the common thread that runs through all of my novels is of a man, or a woman, who finds himself/herself outside of society, maybe even in a state of neurosis, psychosis, or derangement. This last novel has a man and a woman who are psychotic in different ways. What I try to do is always pose the question, "Is this man or woman more abnormal than the 'normal society' around them?" I want the reader to be poised between these two values, and I want the question always to be raised as to who's crazy, whether the psychotic person is crazy, or the outside person—Binx Bolling, the king of laid-back, cool outsider; or Will Barrett, who's a much more disturbed outsider; Lancelot, who's downright violent; and the rather shadowy priest, who is kind of the mirror image of Lancelot. The reader is supposed to recognize the outsider in himself, and to identify with the alienated values of these characters. Maybe I try to design it so that it will cross the reader's mind to question the, quote, "normal culture," and to value his own state of disorientation. You say the search. I think the search is the normal condition. I think that's the one thread which unites all of my characters, that they're at various stages of disorder, and are aware of it, and not necessarily unhappy about it, not altogether unhappy about it.

Jones: Yes, not victims of the worst type of despair.

Percy: Yes.

Jones: I read the short story, the excerpt that you had in *Harper's* from your new novel. I see that you're returning to Will Barrett.

Percy: Yes, that's Will Barrett twenty years later.

Jones: Why Will Barrett?

Percy: I don't know why Will Barrett. I started writing this novel and it wasn't Will Barrett. He had a different name. After hundred pages or so I realized it was Will Barrett; at least with a couple of changes I was able to make it Will Barrett very easily. It couldn't have been anybody else, so I became aware it was Will Barrett.

Jones: Is Will Barrett closer to your own condition?

Percy: I don't know, not necessarily; no closer than Binx, no closer than Thomas More, or even Lancelot, or even the priest. I don't know. Or even Kate. Maybe Kate's closer to me than any of them.

Jones: Talking about Kate, have they ever considered making a movie out of *The Moviegoer*?

Percy: Well, Karen Black bought it, but nothing ever happened. She hasn't made it.

Jones: I can't see her as Kate.

Mrs. Percy: I told her that. It shocked her.

Percy: I made the mistake of saying, "Karen, which secretary are you going to play, Linda or Stephanie or Sharon?" She said, "I'll have you know I'll be playing Kate." She'd be a much better Linda.

Jones: She probably hasn't ever done anything with it because, playing Kate, she couldn't get anybody else involved.

Percy: Well, she had her a leading man lined up.

Mrs. Percy: A great leading man!

Percy: Yes, he would have been all right.

Mrs. Percy: Sam Waterston.

Jones: Yes, Sam Waterston.

Mrs. Percy: He would really be good.

Jones: He'd be a good Binx.

Percy: You know him? He played Nick Carraway in *Gatsby*.

Jones: Yes. I've seen him in other things too.

Percy: No, what happened was she split with her husband, and it was her husband's screenplay. I think she was doing it to help him out, doing it to be nice to him. He was the one that liked it. She didn't care much one way or another. I think, when they split, that was the end of it as far as she was concerned.

Jones: Has anyone else approached you about dramatizing any of your novels?

Percy: Yes.

Jones: *Lancelot?*

Percy: Yes, somebody has an option on *Lancelot*.

Jones: Good. One final question. I met you down at Mandeville where you were meeting with some fellow artists and writers. In a '68 interview I read, you said, "I have a couple of friends who're writers, but I don't talk to them very much." Do you think that it is important that writers communicate with each other?

Percy: Not particularly.

Jones: You remember Cowley said that if Faulkner had

had some friends of like intellect to discuss things with his fiction would have been better.

Percy: No. No, if I thought that, I'd be living in New York, or living up in that Connecticut area where Styron and Updike and Cheever live. I don't think that's too important. In fact, I don't think they see too much of each other, to tell the truth.

Jones: Well, we've talked for a couple of hours and I know you're tired. I just want to say that I appreciate your talking with me and having me down.

Percy: Well, it's been a pleasure, John.

Photograph by John Griffin Jones

Ellen Douglas

October 23, 1980

We'd arranged to meet at her home in Greenville on a weekday afternoon in late October. Her husband answered my knock at the front door, and when she came she was drying her hands on a dishtowel. As she led me through the house to a den I noticed very little to indicate that a working writer was in residence. Indeed, seeing her in work clothes and catching a few good whiffs of the food cooking in her kitchen made me realize the difficult balance of commitments she must maintain as an artist, housewife, and mother. One of her three grown sons was home that day, and I heard the sounds of both rock and classical music emanating from different parts of the house. After we'd talked for ten minutes, I glanced down to see hundreds of feet of tape strewn under my chair. She handled the situation with grace and took the opportunity to make coffee as I rewound the tape by hand. Once the problems had been dealt with, she spoke with clarity and precision to the issues.

Jones: I'm about to interview Mrs. Josephine Haxton. Her pen name is Ellen Douglas. Let's get some of your early background first.

Douglas: I was born in Natchez in July 1921. My parents were living in Arkansas, but both parents' homes were in Natchez, and they were there at the time for a visit. I lived in a little town called Hope, in the southwest part of Arkansas, until I was ten; then we moved to central Louisiana—Alexandria—and lived there until I was out of high school. I went to Randolph-Macon for the first two years and then to Ole Miss for a year and a half. I graduated from Ole Miss in February 1942.

Jones: I thought you grew up in Natchez.

Douglas: No. Both sets of grandparents lived in Natchez, and we usually spent part of our summers there. After I was grown and graduated from college, I worked there and lived with my grandmother for a year or so. I still have close ties there. We own a place out in the country. My son and his wife and children live there.

Jones: The place down there was in the Ayres family?

Douglas: Right.

Jones: What was your father's occupation?

Douglas: He was a civil engineer. He graduated from Ole Miss in civil engineering—in 1909, I believe. Then he went to M.I.T. for a year and got a graduate degree in engineering there. At the time I was born, he was working for the Arkansas highway department. Then we moved to Alexandria, and he was an independent road and bridge builder for a while. He went out of the engineering business in the early '30s: he had difficulties with the Long regime and became a wholesale gasoline dealer.

Jones: And your ties in Greenville came through your marrying Kenneth Haxton?

Douglas: Yes. I married Kenneth toward the end of the war. We'd both been out of college for two or three years. But I met him at Ole Miss.

Jones: Tell me something about your family in Natchez. Are they an old Mississippi family?

Douglas: Yes, both sides of the family. My mother's great-great-grandfather was one of the last Spanish commandants of Fort Concordia, the Spanish fort across from Natchez. My father's family was an early Scottish family. Hendersons and Ayreses moved into Adams County around the end of the eighteenth century.

Jones: We'll talk more about your family when we get into talking about *A Family's Affairs* and your early writing. You came to Greenville when?

Douglas: Late 1945. My husband was in the navy, and at the end of the war he was released. We had a new baby. I'd been staying with my parents while he'd been overseas during the last year of the war. We came to Greenville just before Christmas of '45.

Jones: And did you have a sense at that time that you might want to write?

Douglas: I'd been interested in writing and had been doing some writing from the time I was in the sixth or seventh grade—maybe even earlier than that. I wrote poems and stories in high school. Of course, in college you don't have much time to write anything but required assignments and I didn't, except in creative writing courses. Then when I graduated from college, I did some more writing. I was working for a radio station as a DJ. During the war there was a shortage of male radio announcers. I worked for a while for KALB in Alexandria and for a while for the radio station in Natchez. They used to have great eighteen-inch platters with half-hour programs on them, and all the DJ had to do was to announce the program, read the ads, and then put the platter on. So I had a good deal of time to myself. That was when I started writing again, during those long periods when I'd be sitting at the radio station waiting for the program to be over. I began to write short stories. I worked for a while in the army in an induction center at Camp Livingston out from Alexandria. Then I decided I wanted to see the world, so I went to New York and worked there in a bookstore for a while. Early in '45 I got married.

Jones: So all you had was some brief experience with creative writing courses at that time?

Douglas: No. My writing experience was mainly what I'd done by myself for my own pleasure. After I married, I had three children in rapid succession and had no time for writing, although I did a great deal of reading in those years and some editing of things my husband was working on. I didn't start writing again methodically, seriously, until my youngest child started nursery school. When all my children were out of the house in the morning, when I had the house to myself, I began to write. That was when I was thirty-three, thirty-four.

Jones: And at what point did it become clear to you that your writing might have a wide appeal?

Douglas: At that time I began, as I said, to work seriously and methodically at writing. I didn't have any idea whether or not my work would appeal to anybody. I just began to write stories as well as I could. And I did it because it interested me. Then, before very long, I found it such fascinating work that it would have been hard to stop.

Jones: When you moved to Greenville in 1945, you moved to a place that had a literary legacy. Do you think that living here in Greenville and being around people who were published writers had an influence on you?

Douglas: Of course, I had read *Lanterns on the Levee* and William Alexander Percy's poetry before I came to Greenville. *Lanterns on the Levee* was widely popular in the South. Mr. Percy was dead by the time I got here. I think he died in '42. I never knew him. And the reason I came to Greenville obviously was because I married somebody who came from here. It had nothing to do with the literary tradition. However, in the early years of my marriage, the first three or four years of my marriage, I was exceedingly lucky that Shelby Foote lived here and was already a friend of my husband's and became a good friend of mine. He was methodically reading through the canon of English literature, and, as I began to read, it was grand for me to have Shelby to talk to about what I was reading. It was an enormous plus in my early married life. When I first came here, during 1945 and the early part of 1946, maybe up until the end of '46, Walker Percy was here. He had just come back to Greenville from Saranac. It was before he married. He and Shelby and Kenneth and I used to read plays together. That was fun too. But by the end of the year he was gone. Later Bern and Franke Keating read with us. Other than those contacts with Shelby and Walker, I had no "literary friendships."

Jones: You had always been around people like Mr. Foote and Dr. Percy, to whom literature, art, really mattered? I've always thought that was what was so remarkable about them and the Greenville of their time.

Douglas: No, I had not always been around people like Walker and Shelby. There isn't anybody like either one of them. I did not grow up in a society where the arts were important. Rather, insofar as my childhood was concerned, the church and religion were important; men were expected to enter professions or to be successful in business; and women were expected to be homemakers. There were always books around, but I would say that contemporary art and contemporary serious literature were viewed with suspicion or contempt. At the same time I knew that my parents wanted all their children to use their talents—in the Biblical sense. In adolescence, when I began to choose the world I would live in, I cared about books and was writing fiction, and naturally some of my friends shared these interests.

Jones: During the time we're discussing, Greenville was a town of 15,000 to 20,000 people, and there were seventeen published writers who called Greenville home. Did this literary tradition not mean anything to you?

Douglas: It didn't have the slightest effect on my work. I'm not at all sure whether it even existed. As far as I know, there certainly wasn't any "literary salon." But Hodding Carter was not only a friend but a family connection of mine. We saw something of Hodding and Betty. I worked for him as a researcher and did a lot of reading for him for *The Angry Scar.* Of course we enjoyed them, but I don't think any of that had any effect on his work or mine. His presence here was a direct result of the Percys' interest in having a good newspaper in the town. They and their friends and business associates brought him here. But, no. I don't see any literary connections.

Jones: So, it's just a matter of chance that so many writers were at work in Greenville at that time?

Douglas: I don't mean to say I don't think Mr. Percy influenced people. Walker was his adopted son. And certainly he must have had considerable effect on Dave Cohn. The Percys lived in a world that had a particular tone—that is, a world in which music and literature were important. Probably it's true that there are very few families like that in small Southern towns. And they had their effect on their friends. All I'm saying is that I can't make any connection between the people who actually wrote and published books and those facts about the Percys, other than the connection with Dave Cohn and Shelby and Walker. Of course, Shelby grew up in the Percy house, but on the other hand I think if Shelby had grown up in Timbuktu he would have ended up being some kind of artist because that's his nature—maybe not even a writer, but some other kind of artist. He's deeply interested in music and has a very strong graphic gift. He would have done one thing or another, no matter where he was. But for me—although it sounds strange, it is certainly true—sitting here looking at these books, which are mostly my husband's, reminds me that one of the strong early influences on my work was my husband, in the sense that we were reading together. He was writing; I was thinking about what he was writing and how I would do it if I did it myself and to some degree helping him edit some of the things he was writing. During those years when my children were small, before I began seriously to work on my own things, that was what kept my interest in writing alive. I learned a great deal through the editing and the conversations about motive and characterization.

Jones: Yet Greenville was also a social oddity in Mississippi, wasn't it?

Douglas: I think the Percys had a strong influence on the political and social tone here. Of course if the Percys and their associates hadn't made the stand they did in the '20s (as described in *Lanterns on the Levee*), very likely the Klan would have gotten a stronger hold here. But then there was a large and stable and fairly influential Jewish community here, which, of course, would've been a strong deterrent. It also seems to me that, as is true in a great many Southern cities, the Jewish community here was closely integrated into the gentile community, so that the Jews had a great many friends who would have been opposed to the activities of the Klan. As you know, my husband is half Jewish. His grandfather Blum was a merchant here for many years. (Shelby Foote's grandfather was Jewish, too, incidentally.) By the end of the '50s when things began to get a little ominous in political and social terms, the fact that the Percys had brought the Carters to Greenville had a radical effect on the tone, social and political, of Greenville and made it different from other small towns in the state. The paper was actively concerned that if anybody was in jail there be a good reason for his being there, and if anything illegal happened in the jail, the paper would be on it in a minute. If there were threats against people, they would be exposed in the paper. All this kind of thing made it different from many towns where papers were controlled by reactionary groups.

Jones: Yes. That's true. Could you tell me which writers have influenced your writing?

Douglas: I think writers are usually influenced by the writers of a generation earlier. Certainly I was. When I was very young, I was influenced by Faulkner. I don't think my style is Faulknerian. I had a strong reaction against that influence somewhere along the line—I suppose I got tired of doom—and I wrote in a very different way. But Faulkner was a strong influence, and in a curious way, not only in the power and the overwhelming hypnotic style, but in the sense that he was a writer who was *here.* You recognized that what he had done and what he was doing was something that was needed—and possible—in your own society, and that you might be able to do that kind of thing yourself. It might have seemed very far away from you—unreal—if you had grown up in a little town in Iowa. Of course he was in Oxford when I was at Ole Miss. The great books were coming in those years.

Jones: Did you ever see him?

Douglas: Yes. I saw him occasionally. Oxford was a small town and he was around. I met him once, I think—once then—and then a couple of times in later years. But I never knew him at all. My husband met him on a number of occasions. My husband's father was Cornell Franklin's roommate at Ole Miss (Cornell was Estelle Faulkner's first husband). My father-in-law was a good friend of Estelle's. Kenneth met him several times during the years he was at Ole Miss, and then the Levee Press, in which Kenneth was a partner, brought out *Notes on a Horsethief.*

Jones: What about Miss Welty's influence on you and your writing? Did she have a strong influence?

Douglas: To the degree that I read her short stories and sometimes said a short prayer to somebody that I might write so glitteringly. To that degree—and of course that was important. Looking at her work and the language, how extraordinary it is, it makes you want to emulate it. But to imitate it, no, I never did try. I did imitate Faulkner; I never tried to imitate Miss Welty. I was influenced—I think I was influenced, or at least I was moved by Dostoyevsky, Mann, Conrad in those early years. That's who I was reading. I was influenced to a limited degree by James; that is, I learned a great deal about construction from James. But I suppose Mann and Dostoyevsky and Conrad were the writers I was most moved by in those early years; two of them, of course, in translation. In a sense, when you read the translations, you are not really reading Dostoyevsky, so what I was moved by in each case was a vision of the world.

Jones: The writing of Mann and Dostoyevsky seems to have captured the imagination of your generation of Southern writers. Both Foote and Percy name them as great influences.

Douglas: These writers influenced not just Southern writers but the world. Each of them had an extraordinary synthesizing power—a capacity to write specifically and dramatically about human passion and tragedy in such a way that the individual life expressed truly some part of the significance of human lives in their time and place. For me, too, the writers I've cared most for—these and others—are great storytellers. I care about stories.

Jones: When did you begin your first novel?

Douglas: I was writing short stories, as I said, before I married, but I never did anything about them. Then after Brooks, our youngest son, started nursery school, I went back to them by chance. My husband and I and a friend were talking one night and we made a bet that we'd each write a short story, his position being that he would finish and we wouldn't. I think he probably thought I would, but he didn't think our friend would. And I did. I wrote a short story which eventually became a part of *A Family's Affairs*. Then I began what I thought was a short novel which dealt with another part of the material in *A Family's Affairs*. I put that down and picked up a story I had written before I was married, which dealt with another part of that material, and when I was looking at it, I realized that all three pieces were parts of a novel rather than a series of short stories. That was when I started working on *A Family's Affairs*.

Jones: I've always been interested to talk to writers about what made them sit down to write that first novel. It seems to me that if you're not trying to produce something new in fiction, it would be too intimidating.

Douglas: I don't think that most writers set out to produce something new in fiction. I think what serious writers are doing is trying to say what they mean as clearly and eloquently as they can. If it turns out to be avant-garde or new, that's a by-product. I think you are just trying to say what you mean. And I didn't start working on that novel with anything so specific in mind as "Well, I'm going to finish this book and probably I'll be able to sell it." That seems very unreal and distant to someone who has never had anything published. I was fascinated with what I was doing, and although all along I was hoping somewhere in my head that I might find a publisher, it wouldn't have been something I would have been at all sure of.

Jones: Let me ask you something about your motivation. Richard King recently wrote a book called *Southern Renaissance* dealing with the writers in the South from '25 to '55—Wolfe, Faulkner, Warren and

others—saying essentially that what motivated these
writers was their attempt to come to grips with the
Southern family romance, the truth behind their own
history. I just finished that book this morning, and I
wanted to see what you thought about that argument.
Douglas: That's not the kind of thing I think about.
That's the kind of thing that people who write books
about writers think about. I think that most writers
write to come to terms with and to communicate their
experience. Who can say what produces a phenomenon
like a group of writers in one period, or a group of
composers in one place at one time? It's mysterious.
Certainly—and all of this is trite and has been said
many times by people who say it better than I—the
pressures and hypocrisies and ambiguities of the strange
world that Southerners lived in, and to some degree,
although not nearly so much, still live in, the problems
of race and all the things that are related to the history
of the South, must have had an effect on those writers
who are members of what is called the Southern Renaissance. But take a writer like Flannery O'Connor, for
example. Her obsession is the grace of God. You know?
I think that would have been her obsession no matter
where she lived. So it's hard to make any sweeping
generalizations. Walker Percy's obsession is the Christian wayfarer in the world. At the same time you could
say that he was coming to terms with the family, with
history. But you could not ever say that about O'Connor.
Jones: No, but it struck me as true about so many
Southerners, and you. With your writing there seems
to be an attempt made at coming to grips with the
past.
Douglas: Certainly in the first book.
Jones: Does the evolution of the Southern family interest you anymore? Is the old romantic notion of the
South, and the problems that notion caused, dead to-

day? Especially as material for the Southern writer working in the 1980s?

Douglas: I don't have any intimate experience of English families or Chinese families, so, perforce, I'll always use Southern families in my work. By the same token, the landscape I know is the South and so I'll always use that. I was never much interested in "romantic" fiction about the South—hoop skirts and moonlight. But Stark Young wrote a good novel with all that paraphernalia in it, and who's to say whether it will be useful tomorrow to someone else.

Jones: What makes you sit down and write? Is there something beyond the human condition that you are investigating through your fiction?

Douglas: Shelby says writing is the only thing worth a grown man's time. That's not true, of course, but artists think art is *important*. I care about writing. Insofar as one can give one's life meaning of any kind, making things—art—gives one's life meaning.

Jones: Once I read that Doris Lessing said she had been asked many times about her techniques and her inspiration, but she said, "No one has ever asked me where I got the energy." Where do you get your energy?

Douglas: I write because I'm unhappy if I don't. If I go through a period when a book is not working for me, I'm unhappy, and if I'm writing and it's going well, I'm pleased. The main reason I sit down is that I want to be happy. I want it to work. And once you start doing that, gradually you become obsessed with it. It becomes essential. Then it's not a question of where you get the energy; it's how could you *not* do it? You have to do it because it's what you care about doing, or so it seems to me. As far as physical energy is concerned, it doesn't take very much. Psychic energy is another matter. It does take an immense amount of psychic energy. But it takes an immense amount of psychic energy to be unhappy, too.

Jones: But it would seem to require a great amount of energy, psychic and otherwise, to strip bare one's emotion day after day on the page. That seems to be communicated in the best fiction.

Douglas: Yes. I think an artist has to look at the world (including himself) with a clear and ruthless eye if he hopes to produce anything worth reading—and that's always difficult. We like to believe comfortable lies about ourselves.

Jones: Do you revise extensively?

Douglas: Yes. I revise a great deal. But I like to do that. The business of revision is one of the best parts of writing—making things work, fitting things together. The first draft is what's hard. To get enough down so that you can go back and revise is the hardest part.

Jones: One of the things that King points out in his book is that many Southern writers write so as to put history to rest, to exorcise their bad memories by writing them down. That would seem to me to be difficult.

Douglas: Not so much to exorcise as to make sense of. Making art is an attempt to bring some order to the chaos of one's life, which is another way of saying the same thing.

Jones: When your first work, *A Family's Affairs*, was accepted, were you surprised?

Douglas: I certainly was surprised. I hadn't even sent it off anywhere. I didn't know anybody was looking at it. It was an accident.

Jones: Tell me that story.

Douglas: I had given it to Charles Bell, who was a good friend of mine and my husband's. He was teaching at that time in Annapolis at St. John's. As you know, he's a poet and novelist. I said, "I've finished a draft of this novel I'm working on. Why don't you take it back with you to Annapolis and tell me what you think of it? You don't have to worry about sending it back to me in a hurry because I'm working on something else now and I'm not going to be worrying about it for some months, so just keep it as long as you want to." He took it back with him. Several months went by, and the telephone rang one day, and it was a strange man's voice, New England accent, and it was Craig Wiley, who was at that time a senior editor at Houghton Mifflin. He told me that he had been in Annapolis (Houghton Mifflin later brought out a couple of Charles's novels) and he had spent the night with the Bells, and he was looking for manuscripts for their twenty-fifth anniversary fellowship competition. He had asked Charles if he knew anybody who was working on a novel, and Charles said, "Yes. I've got a novel a friend of mine in Mississippi is working on. Would you like to take it with you?" Wiley was calling to say that he had read it and that he would like for me to enter it in the competition. At the time I hadn't thought what I would do with it. I had not come to that hurdle. I thought of it as an apprentice work, and I knew I had to rewrite it, so I told him that I didn't know whether I wanted to enter it in the competition or not. A day passed. He called back and asked if I had made up my mind and I said, "No." And he said, "Well, we want something of yours in the competition, so if you don't want to enter this, why don't you enter something else? Have you anything else?" And I said, "I have a long short story, a novella really, which is at *The New Yorker* now, but I suppose they're going to reject it." (They'd rejected a couple of my short stories at that time.) He said, "If they reject it, I would like to enter it in the competition. I'm going to call them and see what they're going to do with it." The next day he called and said, "*The New Yorker* is going to accept your story, so we can't use it because our entries have to be unpublished work. So what are you going to do?" I said, "Well, I don't know. I need to do a great deal more work on it." And he said, "If you want me to help you make up your mind, Mrs. Haxton, if you will enter it

in the competition, it has won." So I said, "Well, in
that case . . . ."

Jones: "Okay."

Douglas: Yes. It was an unusual, backwards way to
get published.

Jones: You weren't angry with Charles Bell for giving
away your unfinished manuscript?

Douglas: Certainly not. I presume he thought if I'd
written it I wanted it published. He had a novel in the
same competition, so it was generous of him to give
them mine. He entered *The Married Land,* and Houghton Mifflin did publish *The Married Land.*

Jones: What short story was appearing in *The New
Yorker?*

Douglas: "On the Lake" was the name of it.

Jones: And when was it published?

Douglas: The story in *The New Yorker* came out, I
believe, in '61. The novel came out in '62 or '63, about
a year after the story came out. As I say, it needed
work, and I did work on it for a long time.

Jones: Sixty-two. Same year *The Moviegoer* came out.

Douglas: It came out before *The Moviegoer.*

Jones: Let me ask you about a theme in your work that
is evident from your early work down through *The Rock
Cried Out.* There is an attempt to portray in a realistic
way the relationship between blacks and whites in Mississippi. Perhaps that is the most interesting thing to
me personally in your work. Take "Jesse," for example:
what is interesting is that here is a person—the white
woman—who is trying to treat blacks in a conscientious and moral way during a period of intense racial
strife, who is trying perhaps to convey to the blacks in
the stories that she cares for them without being pa-
tronizing; yet she is still damned. Two hundred years of
history could not be erased in the mind of the black
man by one moderate white. It is the same thing with
Estella in "On the Lake." There was still a price to pay.

Douglas: I think that in both "Jesse" and "On the Lake" one of the main things I was saying was that one pays lip service to a particular moral position, but there is no way to escape the consequences in one's character and life of living in a society that is based on racial prejudice and hatred. That's just true, or it seemed true to me.

Jones: These things happened to you? You have told me your son is a guitar player.

Douglas: I think all writers use their experience. Certainly there was an old man in Greenville who taught guitar. In fact, he told me a story about his childhood. He did teach my second son guitar. But then you take this and that and other things too. In *The Rock Cried Out* the setting was based very closely on a real setting, and the voice of the narrator is to some degree the voice of my youngest son, and some of the events in the book—for example, that somebody lived back in that swamp during the '30s—are facts. But then the story is an invention. I do think you rely heavily on . . . what else do you have but what you know? But it becomes something very different from what it was in the real world.

Jones: So writing is a process combining memory and imagination?

Douglas: And *craft*.

Jones: What is the writer's greatest gift: the clear eye of memory and experience, the imagination needed to see life through another character's eyes, or the skill of perception?

Douglas: Persistence, maybe. The determination and hardheadedness that keep you trying to make things work, trying again and again no matter how many times you fail.

Jones: It must have been hard on an artist here in Mississippi during the period you are dealing with in *The Rock Cried Out*. So much of that must have been a reflection of some kind of moral outrage you must have felt during that period. How did that affect you?

Douglas: Hard on everybody—especially blacks and civil rights workers. Obviously it affected me, since I used those materials, particularly in *The Rock Cried Out.* Greenville was a much more peaceful community than that fictional community. Nobody bothered us. Life was better here. But of course I was affected. When I have the boy in *The Rock Cried Out* say that a memory from his childhood is of his father opening the paper to see what terrible thing had happened down the road, not in Birmingham or Dallas but in Itta Bena or Greenwood or Chickasaw, I was thinking of myself, because that is what it was like, you know, to open the *Commercial [Appeal]* every morning and see what terrible thing might have happened the day before. One always had a gnawing guilt, or I did, because I wasn't particularly an activist of any kind. I didn't do any of a number of things I might have done to influence events, although I don't think I would have had much influence. That was a source of guilt to a great many people all over the state, and certainly it was to me, too. It was a hard time. It was a bad time. It's hard to believe that young people in their early twenties now hardly even remember it, know nothing about it. My students now have no conception of how things were then, how fantastic, how absurd things were.

Jones: And it plays a part in your art.

Douglas: That's right.

Jones: And to a larger degree than it does in Walker Percy's art or Shelby Foote's art.

Douglas: Certainly in *The Rock Cried Out* it was one of the major things I was interested in.

Jones: Percy says that one of the worst things for an artist or novelist to do is to get too involved in political and social concerns, mass movements and such. Is this something you are conscious of?

Douglas: I don't know how you can generalize about that. Goodness knows somebody like Dickens, for example, was deeply concerned with political reform. Certainly Tolstoy and Dostoyevsky were insane on the subject of religion and Pan-Slavism and all kinds of political and religious questions. I know Walker has said that as soon as a novel becomes didactic, as soon as the writer's intent is didactic, it will kill the novel. But how can you even say that much? To some degree *his* intent is didactic. I think that if a novel is good, it's good, and if it's bad, it's bad, and those things don't matter very much. It all depends on one's power, the power of one's conception and one's ability to execute it. I think, for example, that in *The Last Gentleman*—the long business of Sutter's notebook—it is hard to see that that has anything but a didactic purpose. It is the same in *The Magic Mountain* in the long conversation between Settembrini and the Jesuit. But if the novel can contain it and survive, then it does. And if it can't contain it and survive, then it doesn't.
Jones: Well, again, that's why I liked *The Rock Cried Out* so much. It is one of the first times I have read a long fictional account of the movements of those days.
Douglas: I think what happened to me as far as *The Rock Cried Out* is concerned is that I got interested in the sensibility of the young people who grew up in that period. It was a generation I knew a lot about, since I knew my sons and their friends and cousins and girlfriends. It seemed to me to be a period that I was well equipped to consider, since I had spent a great deal of time listening to those young people talk. And if you're going to deal with that group, the political situation is one of the things you consider. I decided I wanted to write a book about that generation of young people; and the movement, the Vietnam War, the civil rights struggle were *there*. You used them to construct a story. I am a novelist who likes to read good stories and who tries to write good stories, exciting stories.

Jones: That is important to you?

Douglas: Yes.

Jones: It's more structured and plotted than is *A Family's Affairs*.

Douglas: *A Family's Affairs* is a loosely-put-together book. I think it works in its own way. But I was interested in plot in *The Rock Cried Out*, in fitting all the material together and making it work.

Jones: Let me ask you this question about an artist's obligation to what he's writing about: if *Apostles of Light* is an indictment of the way we treat old people, and indeed everything we don't like to look at in society, did that intention ever translate itself into your working with a reform effort?

Douglas: No. Although I think that's wonderful for those who—I mean, that's a necessary thing to do. I'm not a very strongly political person. I vote. I support candidates I believe I should support. But I'm not much of a joiner of movements. I tend to go my solitary way. I think that's not unusual for a writer. It's a solitary profession.

Jones: It seems as if you would have been contacted by people who were interested in improving nursing homes.

Douglas: No, neither before nor after I wrote the book, and my interest in the subject came about in a very immediate way out of the private world that I live in. My husband had been the only child, the only grandchild on both sides of his family, and there were a number of aunts and uncles who had no children, no other relatives to help take care of them in their old age. Therefore I spent many hours in the years just prior to *Apostles of Light* visiting this or that old relative in this or that nursing home. That's what got me thinking about the predicament of old people. Then, when I decided to do the book, I imagined a very eccentric nursing home, to say the least. It was not at all like the ones I used to visit here.

Jones: It must have been a hard book to write.

Douglas: You mean distressing?

Jones: Yes. That's a little too much reality almost.

Douglas: Yes. Well, by the time one writes, one hopes one is detached from the material. For example, the story "On the Lake" is based fairly closely, although it's changed radically in some places, on something that did happen to me and a black woman who went fishing with me and my children. At the time that it happened it would have been too distressing to write about. It was several years before I considered using the material. By the time I used it, I had gone over and over it in my mind, and it had acquired a life of its own detached from my personal life. Or I hope it had. It had become an artistic problem and not a personal one. That's true of *Apostles of Light*. Certainly we had some distressing experiences with my husband's aunt, but by the time I wrote about them I was detached and it was not about *that* person.

Jones: About the accident in "On the Lake," was there a man who came down and helped you?

Douglas: Yes. But not *that* man. The character of the man who rescued the people in the story was based fairly closely on the character of a friend of mine. But he didn't happen to rescue us. I just used his appearance and character. A black man helped us.

Jones: And did the black woman have water in her lungs?

Douglas: Yes, we thought she was dead. That was very close to what I wrote.

Jones: And a water moccasin ate the fish?

Douglas: No, no. All that—the picnic, everything— was arranged for the purpose of the story, not at all on the basis of what happened.

Jones: Yes.

Douglas: I have had a water moccasin eat my fish though—a turtle, too.

66

Jones: You enjoy fishing and fish a lot, don't you?

Douglas: I used to; I don't fish much anymore, for several reasons. Lake Ferguson is not as attractive as it used to be. For another thing, I am getting older and I can't carry a motor as easily as I used to. For a third thing, my children are all grown now, and they were the ones I would enlist to go put the motor on the boat for me and help me get off. I fish when I go to Natchez to visit my son. He lives in the country and has several ponds close to his house. I fish in them when I'm down there.

Jones: What about the character Harper in *Apostles of Light*? Have you ever known a black man who had no formal education, who was self-schooled, yet had ideas of that caliber?

Douglas: No. And I didn't say that he was entirely self-taught. Didn't I say that he had gone off to college? I think I did. I based the character to a limited degree on a black man I knew. I stretched it. I got the idea for his obsession with caves and hiding places out of my head. It was an idea that was useful to me only in terms of the book. I did know a black man who was fairly well educated but had done it for himself. But I changed his character radically. I could use him again. He's a wonderful character.

Jones: He is.

Douglas: No, I don't mean Harper. I mean the real man, who's long dead now, was a fantastic character. I could use him in another way in another book. He was a terrible snob.

Jones: Did he appear somewhat in *The Rock Cried Out* as Noah?

Douglas: No, no. Noah's physical appearance is a bit like Jesse's physical appearance. In both cases I used the same man for the long, gaunt body and the long jaw. There was a little alteration, but I used the same physical man for those two black characters, although not at all, obviously, the same circumstances or lives or personalities. Harper was based on another man. And his circumstances were all made up. All the events were.

Jones: And *The Rock Cried Out?*

Douglas: Oh, yes, that's all made up. You know, the plot and story were all made up.

Jones: Where did you get the idea for *The Rock Cried Out?*

Douglas: As I said earlier, my original intent was to explore the sensibility of young people of my children's generation. When I decided to do that, I then had to decide where to put them, and it occurred to me that the setting in rural south Mississippi would be extraordinarily fruitful in terms of producing the kinds of circumstances that I could use in making that exploration, particularly because that part of the country was violently involved in the civil rights movement. I also knew the isolated, rural world I wanted to use; I was at home there. I knew the kind of people I would use, both the young white people and the black families. I had had some experience—very limited—with Pentecostal or charismatic white Christian people. I decided I'd use the need for conversion as the turning point of the book. I had already created the character of Dallas and the character of Lindsey Lee on the basis of young men I had known—combinations of some characteristics of young men I had known. And then when I decided to use a charismatic Christian conversion, I started going to church and made myself at home in that idiom. So that's the way it was.

Jones: And did you find one of those fundamentalist churches?

Douglas: You don't have to go far to find one. There are a number of them in town. I went to church here, and I went to church in Alexandria. At that time my mother was still alive and lived there, and I went to church when I was visiting her.

Jones: And Alan, the young, prideful, artistic boy?

Douglas: As I said earlier, to some degree I used the voice of my youngest son, who is, in fact, a poet. Again, as I said, the story is not about him. The story is made up. I used my sons as walking encyclopedias when I was writing that book. I could always go to them and say, "I want to say this. Does this ring true?" My middle son is a welder and carpenter and a country man, and he was really an encyclopedia.

Jones: Yes, as Alan built that house.

Douglas: They were useful to me. But the book is not in any way connected with their lives, except that they did restore an old house on the place. At one time or another all three of them worked on it.

Jones: Did you enjoy writing that book more than any other book because you could involve your sons in it?

Douglas: I had a terrible time with that book. I had two long dry spells. It was exceedingly hard to put together. The problems of making the plot work convincingly were difficult. There were several periods of months and months when I would try one thing and it wouldn't work and try another thing and it wouldn't work. In that sense it was a difficult book to write. The last year, when it was going well and I was confident that it was going to come together, I enjoyed working on it. I felt good about it when I finished it. I felt I had made a step, had done something a little bit different.

Jones: One thing I was interested in asking you was about using characters who came of age in the '60s and '70s in fiction. Does the fact that kids of that generation were so heavily influenced by the social and political forces you've already mentioned make them harder to write about, any less singular or separable, than kids of an earlier generation? Barry Hannah's *Geronimo Rex* and Jim Whitehead's *Joiner* have protagonists who are of that period. Is it more difficult to write about people from this later period?

Douglas: The extreme pressures of the period make it a good period for the novelist, because the novelist is always concerned with individual behavior under pressure. As for my own guilt, I think the world I grew up in was considerably stabler. But it was a kind of backwater in a larger world where all the forces that have produced the fragmentation of the present were already at work.

Jones: Has *The Rock Cried Out* sold better than *Apostles of Light*?

Douglas: I don't think it has. It sold fairly well. I'm not sure how many copies *Apostles of Light* sold. Unfortunately I'm not a very big seller. I'm a modestly successful writer. But it has sold paperback rights. I never did sell paperback rights for *Apostles of Light*. Ballantine is going to bring out the paperback probably sometime in the next few months.

Jones: What about the scene where Dallas pours out his heart over the CB radio? Did it take you a long time to come up with a scene in which Dallas could be revealed?

Douglas: One of the major difficulties I had in putting that book together was the presentation of characters other than Alan. I wanted Alan's to be the dominant voice. I wanted the reader to have a strong sense of Calhoun Levitt and Noah and of Dallas. Early on I thought of using a CB radio for Dallas's confession. In fact—something I rarely do—I wrote the confession when I was only about halfway through the book, and then went back and wrote up to it. You can see the difficulties I would have had if I had had Alan reporting to the reader what Dallas had confessed. So the CB radio and the tapes worked out well. At least it seemed to me that they worked.

Jones: What about bringing things to a head at the end, having a dramatic climax? Many new novels don't have the big ending anymore, and, as in life most of the time, the reader is left with hints and possibilities rather than clear statements about the fate of the characters.

Douglas: The end of *The Rock Cried Out* is left open in the sense that the reader has only *Alan's* view of what his life will be like. On the basis of the presentation of the character, there are other possibilities. Clearly, he's changed, learned *something,* but the world with all its difficulties lies before him.

Jones: You mentioned earlier that there was a couple who lived in the woods in the 1930s, a girl with long beautiful hair . . .

Douglas: Yes, an old black man who lived down there told me the story of this mysterious couple. He was a fine storyteller, and he told the story to me years ago, at least fifteen years ago. I knew I would use it. It just stayed in my head until I used it. I made up all the surrounding circumstances. He didn't know where they came from or where they were going. The murder was made up too. They were not murdered. They simply vanished. But I was intrigued with the story he told me about the way they treated him, which was very like the way the couple in the book treated Calhoun. He said they loaded up their old car in the spring and left, and he never knew where they had gone after that. But from the circumstances, I put together my story of their background in the labor movement and the church.

Jones: Let me ask you a couple of final questions. When and how did you get your pen name Ellen Douglas? Nobody knew who Ellen Douglas was for your first couple of books, did they?

Douglas: Not very many people. But I gave that up. Ellen was my grandmother's name—Ellen Henderson Ayres. When I decided I would use a pen name, I used her name because, in fact, she was a writer, of children's stories and romances—mostly not published. She wrote children's stories and read them to us as children.

So I decided to use her given name for my pen name.
My publisher had a son named Douglas, and he suggested that I use Douglas. Both he and I had forgotten
at the time that the Lady of the Lake was named Ellen
Douglas, but, of course, she was.

Jones: And how long was your identity unknown?

Douglas: Not very many people knew who I was when
the first book came out, although Hodding Carter immediately identified me as author of "On the Lake" in
The New Yorker. By the time the second one came out,
most people knew.

Jones: But you didn't put out a news release or anything.

Douglas: No, no.

Jones: Is your mother still alive?

Douglas: No, she died a few years ago.

Jones: I was wondering what she thought of your
fiction, especially as it pertained to the family?

Douglas: Well, of course she never read *The Rock Cried
Out*. She died before I finished it. I don't think she
would've liked it much. She was very conservative. But
she was a great reader. She liked my books.

Jones: Did she like *A Family's Affairs*?

Douglas: Yes, she liked it very much. She was proud
of me.

Jones: As a writer, have you ever been approached by
anyone who said, "No, this part is entirely wrong. This
is not what the black experience in Mississippi is."

Douglas: Once in a while. Occasionally. I don't get
much fan mail, or much nonfan mail either. I did get a
letter from a lady after *The Rock Cried Out* about how
immoral it was. Another lady approached me once and
said she thought it was not possible that a love affair
could have taken place between Leila and Sam. Other
than that, on the other books, no. Oh, yes, I did have a
woman say to me that it was impossible for a black
woman to be buried in a white cemetery. I'd forgotten

that. But that fictional fact was based on the real fact that a black woman is buried in a white cemetery in a Southern town. I am sure there are a great many, of course. In Oxford, I think, Faulkner's mammy was buried in the Faulkner lot.

Jones: Are you working on a novel now?

Douglas: Yes. I had a dry spell after *The Rock Cried Out*, but I began work this summer and have been working since.

Jones: I want to thank you for doing this tape with me, for having me up, and for the coffee, and, especially, your patience.

Douglas: I always enjoy talking about myself. Thank you.

Photograph by Alen MacWeeney

Willie Morris

December 4, 1980

I left a message with his maid for him to call me at the Gin Restaurant in Oxford when he awoke from a late afternoon nap. I was playing shuffleboard with a friend when the call came an hour later. Willie Morris sounded refreshed, downright jaunty, on the telephone. "Hurry on over," he said, "and tell the Mayor we'll be down as soon as we finish the interview." At his house on Faculty Row I was greeted by his old dog Pete, an overweight black lab who wheezed and managed a few indifferent woofs to welcome me, and by Morris, the wayfaring Yazoo boy, looking fit and happy in the appropriate campus clothing: knit sports shirt with "Ole Miss Rebels" printed over the pocket, slacks and penny loafers. The three of us repaired to his sparsely furnished den—a photo of Miss Welty was all that adorned the walls—and there we sat and talked for almost two hours. Afterwards we headed to the Gin where the Mayor was saving us two seats, and late into the night I watched as the author of *North Toward Home* talked with students and locals, signed napkins for sorority girls, and immersed himself in the lively atmosphere of Faulkner's town at the end of a college semester. "You know," he told me just before we parted,

"I'm so glad to be back. Just keep your eyes open; there's so much to see. 'South Toward Home' is coming."

Jones: You say for the last couple of days you've been in Jackson and Yazoo City?

Morris: Yes. Larry Wells of Yoknapatawpha Press in Oxford brought out a fancy reprint of a children's book that I did in about 1970, called *Good Old Boy*. So we were in Yazoo City signing books at the library. And then we went out and had a historic occasion in Belzoni in the Delta. It was the first time an author had ever signed books in Belzoni.

Jones: They don't have a bookstore, do they?

Morris: No, they don't have a bookstore in Belzoni, but they do have a library. Thank God for that.

Jones: And you saw Bubba Barrier?

Morris: I saw my old friend Bubba. I grew up with Bubba, who's your cousin. He was the best man in my wedding.

Jones: Was he?

Morris: Yes, in Houston, Texas, many years ago. The marriage didn't last, but Bubba did. I've known Bubba since we were both about—well, it goes back before memory—since we were about one year old. My first memory of Bubba is a long-ago afternoon. I was killing ants on the sidewalk with a hammer. Bubba said, "The Lord ain't gonna like that." And I guess He didn't.

Jones: Some of my favorite parts of *Good Old Boy* and *North Toward Home* are when you talked about driving around in his red—what did he have, a Model T?

Morris: He had a Model T, yes. One of those old models with a rumble seat. Of course, when we were growing up in Yazoo City, we all started driving when we were about twelve or thirteen. I think Bubba started driving when he was eleven. He'd borrow the family car—his parents didn't know it—and come down and pick me up, and we'd drive all over Brickyard Hill and out into the Delta. I do think Bubba was eleven or twelve then.

Jones: Is Muttonhead Shepherd still alive?

Morris: At last report he is. I sure hope so.

Jones: Where is he?

Morris: Someone told me he's teaching school and coaching up in North Carolina.

Jones: And Honest Ed Upton?

Morris: Honest Ed Upton is a Methodist preacher.

Jones: Where?

Morris: Out in Dallas, Texas. And Big Boy Wilkinson—I saw him the other day in Memphis. He's a very successful dentist in Memphis. So the group seems to be doing okay.

Jones: Did you keep up with them through the years?

Morris: Well, off and on, sporadically. Since I've come back down here to live a good part of the year, I hear a lot about them. So it's an expression of keeping in touch.

Jones: Do you still have family in Mississippi?

Morris: No, I don't. All of my family is dead, except for my son David, who just turned twenty-one. My mother died about three years ago. She was an only child. My grandmother died about six years ago.

Jones: Harper?

Morris: Yes, she came from the Harper family at Raymond. Her father, my great-grandfather, was George W. Harper, who was the editor and publisher of the *Hinds County Gazette* in Raymond. It was one of the distinguished newspapers in the pre-Civil War period. He was one of the first white men reelected to the Mississippi State Senate.

Jones: During Reconstruction?

Morris: Yes. George W. Harper married Anna Sims, from Port Gibson. My grandmother was the youngest of seventeen children, and she was the last one to die.

She's buried in the old section of the cemetery in Raymond, which is crumbling now, and all grown over with vicious weeds. Her grave is about fifty yards from where the Confederate dead are buried. But all my Mississippi people are gone. I've got some relatives up in Tennessee on my father's side.

Jones: Did your father have brothers?

Morris: Yes, he had one brother and three sisters. One of his sisters is still alive. My father was from Camden, Tennessee, which is in Benton County about eighty miles north of Memphis. His parents died when he was a little boy and he was brought up by relatives. His father served in the Tennessee State Senate with Cordell Hull. He was a Tennessean. But my Mississippi roots go back very far. Cowles Mead, who was one of the early territorial governors, was related. So was Henry S. Foote, who was a governor and senator before the Civil War and then in the Confederate Congress.

Jones: He left the Confederacy.

Morris: Yes, toward the end of the war. There's a letter that exists from Lincoln to Grant telling Grant to let ex-Senator Foote come through the lines in Virginia. He became an emigré. He went to Canada after the Civil War.

Jones: So somehow you're connected with Shelby Foote.

Morris: You know, most of the older families in Mississippi are related one way or another. Shelby and I've got to be distant cousins, I would think. The other day in Memphis I met probably the most beautiful girl I've ever met in my life, Lynda Lee Mead Shea, who was Miss America from Ole Miss in about 1962, I suppose. I was signing books in a big bookstore, and she appeared from nowhere—a brief apparition.

Jones: Where's she from?

Morris: She's from Meadville and Natchez, I think, and so we must have shared this same great-great-uncle

Cowles Mead. Meadville was named after Cowles Mead, so we have to be about twentieth cousins. She was so beautiful she frightened me. Baudelaire once wrote a poem many years ago in Paris, describing his fortuitous meeting with a girl so beautiful she frightened him. Why did she scare him so much, he asked in his own poem. She frightened him about the possibilities of his own capacity for love, he said to himself, and all the complexities of such things. Then, suddenly, in the bookstore in Memphis, this girl vanished for me, like a pebble in a pond. Just as well. We're still cousins, I'll bet. Anyway, I'm not really sure she was there. She was a dream, that's all. It was a Mississippi thing, even in Memphis.

Jones: A vision. Did your daddy come down here to work because your mother wanted to be near her family?

Morris: No. They actually met in Jackson. My daddy came down here during the Depression and went to work for Standard Oil in Jackson. That building still stands—that old office building right across from the War Memorial. Anyway, my mother and father met in the late '20s. They moved to Yazoo City when I was about six months old, in 1935.

Jones: I was reading some of the newspaper clippings on *North Toward Home*, and I read where some Yazoo Citian wrote in: "Why doesn't Jackson claim Willie Morris? He was born there."

Morris: That Yazoo person didn't want me, I guess. Many people in Yazoo City were upset when *North Toward Home* came out. I knew they would be, but they're not anymore. I think they were mad at me for about five or six years. But this always happens in America with writers. In your home town they get a little disturbed at first when a book comes out that deals with people there, whether it's fictitious or not. *North Toward Home*, of course, was an autobiography.

Then they calm down about it. This happens time and again. They grow rather proud of you, in a curious way. It certainly happened here with Faulkner. Lord knows, Sinclair Lewis in Sauk Center, Minnesota—they wouldn't let him back for twenty years.

Jones: They told Thomas Wolfe they'd lynch him if he ever came back to Asheville.

Morris: That's right. Now the tourists all go to his gravestone with the angel on top. I was once in Sauk Center, Minnesota, and I made a point to go to Sinclair Lewis Boulevard. The sign there on Main Street is not just "Main Street," it's "The *Original* Main Street."

Jones: I remember my mother gave me *North Toward Home* when I was fifteen or sixteen, and I read it and thought, "What a wonderful book." I talked to my relatives in Yazoo City about it soon afterwards—not the Barriers—and I was interested to see them look away and half-smile. They said, "Well, you know Willie could've come back here, but he didn't. He should've had the courage to write it living here." That sort of thing.

Morris: Well, I think I probably couldn't have written it living there. It's that old question of where a writer feels he should live. I couldn't live in Yazoo City. You know I love Yazoo City, I have many friends there, but I don't think I can ever work there. I know it too well. And they know me too well. Too many ghosts for all of us. This is the perfect compromise for me, living here in Oxford, with Ole Miss here. Oxford is a hill country town, but there're great similarities between Oxford and Yazoo City, so this is a healthy modus vivendi.

Jones: At the time you were working on *Yazoo: Integration in a Deep Southern Town*, had the town accepted you again, were you able to move freely in the white community?

Morris: Very much so. I talked to anybody I wanted to, from John Satterfield, the lawyer, former president of the American Bar Association, to William Barbour, a friend of mine who probably represents the moderate-conservative establishment in Yazoo City. Of course I had this entree with the blacks, which was necessary.

Jones: At the time you were growing up in Yazoo City, did you have any sense that what you wanted to do was write?

Morris: I think it was a feeling that grew on me over a period of time. I don't think I ever said to myself explicitly, "I want to be a writer." But I was always writing. I had a little portable typewriter I got when I was twelve or thirteen years old, and I started writing sports for the *Yazoo Herald* and for the school paper, and I never stopped. I once quoted Keats' *Ode on a Grecian Urn* in my description of a basketball game between Yazoo City and Satartia. I guess—it's hard to remember these important things—it was at the University of Texas when I was editor-in-chief of the *Daily Texan*, which I think by then was almost without peer the greatest college newspaper in the country. It might have been then that I decided, or maybe it was when I got to Oxford, England, to Oxford University, which I call now the "other Oxford," that I began to have the feeling that I was going to be a writer. I know I started a novel over there in Oxford. I started it after my son David was born in Oxford in 1959. I would stay up all night, and my son was just beginning to crawl. He'd be crawling around the floor of this old Victorian house we lived in, and I'd be writing away on this novel. But I didn't get anywhere with that novel. I burned it.

Jones: Set in Yazoo City?

Morris: Well, set in the Delta, as I recall. I did get a few little things from it here and there in *North Toward Home*. But I think I wrote three novels that I burned over a period of time.

Jones: During what point in your writing life?

Morris: Ten or fifteen years ago. Sometimes you have

to burn them in self-defense. I know a lot of good writers who burned their words. Of course, I wouldn't do that now. Time is too precious. If you burn a manuscript at age forty-six, you'd just as well be a staff writer for *People* magazine.

Jones: Did you destroy these after *North Toward Home?*

Morris: I think one was before, and one was after, when I left *Harper's* magazine in 1971, and moved out to the east end of Long Island to a little town called Bridgehampton. That's been almost ten years.

Jones: Was there anybody in Yazoo City that influenced you in your writing life, that was an intellectual mentor for you in Yazoo City?

Morris: Well, I had a great high school English teacher, Mrs. Omi Parker. I saw her yesterday, as a matter of fact. I dedicated this new edition of my children's book *Good Old Boy* to her. She was a marvelous high school English teacher, and a genuine taskmaster who opened up to me the whole world of language and its possibilities. She got us to reading good books, literature, and poetry. Then I guess the *Yazoo Herald* under the Motts was always good to me. But in general I think it was the whole atmosphere of growing up in a town like Yazoo City, half hills and half delta, and all crazy, that must have brought out certain impulses.

Jones: When did you get your political education, become aware politically?

Morris: At the University of Texas. There's a fellow out there named Ronnie Dugger who had founded the *Texas Observer*, a really great little paper. It was a weekly at that time. I came under the influence of Ronnie, who was a politically active, brilliant young man several years older than I. I'd never been political before. I do remember I wrote an editorial in the Yazoo High *Flashlight* in 1948 endorsing the Dixiecrat ticket—Strom Thurmond and Fielding L. Wright, the Mississippi governor. But I became rather political there at the University of Texas running the highly controversial student newspaper, the *Daily Texan.* I then went off to Oxford, England, for four years and then came back and took over the *Texas Observer,* a political and literary journal. I think for a writer the best thing about that experience was moving about among different kinds of people, and traveling around Texas and writing a lot of words under a deadline, thousands of words every week. That was probably the toughest job I ever had, the *Texas Observer.* After my tenure running that, I was exhausted. It was a lot harder than running *Harper's,* because at *Harper's* I had good people working with me, and it was a monthly. You had the great writers contributing. But the *Texas Observer* was a marvelous experience, writing constantly about that vast and unusual state.

Jones: As editor of the *Daily Texan* as an undergraduate, did you think about returning to Mississippi and getting into journalism?

Morris: As a matter of fact, I remember some thoughts I had along those lines in Oxford, England, later. I expected to stay there two years and I ended up staying four. I got married in my third year. But I remember I wrote big Hodding Carter with the Greenville paper during my last months in England asking him if he had any jobs. He didn't at the time. I did come back to this country in the summer of 1958 and worked with Ronnie Dugger on the *Texas Observer.* Ronnie was getting tired, and he asked me to return from England and take over the paper from him. Subsequently I did that. But I certainly did have strong temptations to come back to Mississippi after England.

Jones: I've heard you say that you thought for a time about coming back and entering Mississippi politics.

Morris: Well, I think I did have some thoughts about that. I guess if I'd done that I would've come back to the Ole Miss law school and would've had quite a different life. But I don't know. I eventually stayed with the written word, and I don't have too many regrets about that.

Jones: Was Mississippi something that you felt you needed to leave at the time that you left it?

Morris: I don't think it was that conscious. One can look back over one's life and give a rationale to things that I don't think often exists in reality. You know, in retrospect you can give some kind of coherent pattern to your life, but the big decisions are often so—not haphazard—but often the creature of accident. It depends so much on the moment. But I'm glad I went back to Texas after England. I wouldn't take anything for that experience on the *Observer* and an atrocious one several months later in a place called Palo Alto, California.

Jones: Doing what?

Morris: My ex-wife had a Woodrow Wilson Fellowship and was doing graduate work in English.

Jones: At Stanford?

Morris: Yes. As I recall she had a choice between Stanford and Columbia, and we decided that we'd go out to Stanford because we'd never live on the West Coast in the natural course of things. I had a suspicion that we were going to end up in New York City anyway. I remember we were sitting at the breakfast table in Austin, Texas, one morning. I was running the *Texas Observer*, and I'd been doing some writing for *Harper's* when John Fischer was the editor. Suddenly with the morning mail came this letter from Fischer, editor of *Harper's* for a number of years. I must have been twenty-five years old, maybe twenty-six, and here was this letter from John Fischer saying quite frankly that he was looking for a successor, that he was getting tired and he liked my writing, liked the *Texas Observer*, and wondered if I would come up to New York and take a job as associate editor, and then if I worked out I would be his successor. That's a very unusual letter to get in the morning mail in Austin, Texas, when you're twenty-five, twenty-six.

Jones: Why haven't we, your readership, heard more about your experiences in Oxford?

Morris: I have down in the basement of this house a pretty good segment of a novel set in Oxford, England, about between 40,000 and 50,000 words. Actually I'm under contract now for two novels with Doubleday. One of the books is a novel set in Oxford, England. I hope I can find the cardboard box it's in. The other is the one I'm working on now, called *Taps*.

Jones: *Taps*.

Morris: I think what I'll do when I finish *Taps* is go back to that Oxford book, because I like it. It begins in Chapel Hill, North Carolina. I have a first-person protagonist who's a North Carolinian, and one of the characters is somebody from the Mississippi Delta. It begins as a love story. My title is *The Chimes at Midnight*, which is from Shakespeare. It's from a conversation between Falstaff and Master Shallow walking along the old city wall at midnight when all the bells start ringing. Oxford is such an exotic experience for young Americans. There have been many talented Americans at Oxford University over the years, some splendid writers. I once asked Red Warren—Robert Penn Warren—if he'd ever written anything based on his years in Oxford, and he said he'd never been able to get even a short poem out of it. You go there and you're thrown into another world. My college, New College, was founded in 1386. You're living in a museum. You're overwhelmed with this horrendous sense of the past, and then all of a sudden you're back in your own country to make your way, and it's immensely hard to work all that in. When I was writing *North Toward Home* I did try to bring Oxford in. I divided that book into three parts: "Mississippi, Texas, New York." I probably should've had another section called, "America Abroad," or "America From Abroad," or some such, and I should've tried to wrench something about Oxford out of me for that. But I didn't do it. Maybe I'll get this novel done. Anyway, it's one of those things.

Jones: Robert Penn Warren was a Rhodes Scholar?

Morris: Red's from Guthrie, Kentucky. I'm trying to get him down to Ole Miss this spring with his best friend, William Styron.

Jones: I saw you and William Styron at Millsaps [College] with the governor last spring. That's where I met you for the first time. What were you doing over there at Oxford, studying to get a master's?

Morris: Yes, I got a B.A., but at Oxford if you get a B.A., it automatically becomes a master's after several years.

Jones: Why did you spend four years there?

Morris: Well, I think toward the end I was looking for a scholarship with a built-in retirement plan.

Jones: With a pension.

Morris: You get so lazy over there. Nobody ever tells you what to do. I started out in a program called Philosophy, Politics, and Economics: PPE. I didn't like that too much. I couldn't deal with the British linguistic philosophy; it drove me quite mad. It didn't seem to make any sense to me. At first I thought I was dumb, then decided otherwise. So I switched to history. I always loved history. The core of history at Oxford was British history, with a touch of European history. I did a deeply intensive special course in American history covering the decade before the Civil War, which fascinated me.

Jones: The decade of the 1850s.

Morris: Yes, with Arthur Link who had the Harmsworth chair there. Herbert Nicholas, the British historian, was in charge of it. That awakened me to the history of my own country. So I spent another year there officially doing a graduate degree in American-British diplomacy in the ten or fifteen years before World War II.

Jones: Must have had A. J. P. Taylor.

Morris: No. I had Herbert Nicholas. But that was an excuse for me to stay on for another year and read anything I wanted to. The very year I got married the trustees of the Rhodes scholarships voted to allow third-year Rhodes scholars to get married and have their money. So my timing was bad. I borrowed some money from my parents. The warden at Rhodes House, a wonderful man named E. T. "Bill" Williams, who had been General Montgomery's chief of intelligence in World War II, got me my Rhodes money. I was there for my fourth year, and he called it my third. I was reading books and starting a novel that year.

Jones: You came back to Austin one summer during your study and heard from Ronnie Dugger that he was getting tired?

Morris: Yes, that was the summer of 1958. I came back that summer, worked for Ronnie, and got married. So I had a fairly good idea that I'd go back and take over the *Observer* from Ronnie.

Jones: That's a real interesting thing to happen to someone so young. Did you ever consider teaching at that time in your life?

Morris: When I left the *Texas Observer*, I was becoming immersed in American history. When we were out at Stanford, I met the distinguished American historian, David Potter. One of my heroes among the historians was C. Vann Woodward.

Jones: A great Southern historian.

Morris: I later got to know C. Vann Woodward pretty well, a wonderful man. I think for a while I conceived of myself as sort of a C. Vann Woodward of my generation. But I wouldn't have lasted in academia. I have very mixed feelings about academia.

Jones: The other voice you might hear on this tape will be Pete, Mr. Morris's black lab who talks from time to time.

Morris: He's damned articulate, Pete. He's considerably more articulate than some of these Ole Miss coeds. Aren't you, Pete?

Jones: So you returned to the *Texas Observer.* I'm interested to ask you this: here was someone who'd grown up in Yazoo City, Mississippi, certainly a good example of the conservative Deep South, going to work on this muckraking periodical that was certainly concerned with liberal causes; how did you make that leap?

Morris: That's a good question. I think it started at the University of Texas, running the *Daily Texan.* I could argue that the roots of Southern liberalism are deep. The *Observer* was a muckraking paper in the sense that we used investigative reporting, which Lord knows Texas needed, and still does. But it was more than that. The *Observer* had a strong literary side to it. As an editor I don't think I was as political as Ronnie Dugger. It was during my tenure on the *Observer* that I became more and more interested in the human aspect of things. There's a danger when writers get too deeply immersed in politics. This is not to say that writers should not be on the side of civilization, civilizing values, and all the rest. But there is a subtle danger to it, when you involve yourself too much in it. A writer, by the nature of the calling, has to be somewhat detached from himself and from life. You have to have that quality in your perception that makes you a stranger to the things and places and people you care for most. You have to be something of a stranger to the things you love the most. It has to be that way.

Jones: As editor of the *Observer* you had seen the causes come and go and had taken sides?

Morris: Yes. I was very much involved in that. There were aspects of Texas that repelled my Mississippi soul:

the terrible extremes of poverty and wealth and the
callousness of the oil and gas culture would offend any
Southern boy from the Delta, believe me. It was a
rapacious society. I don't think it's any accident that
the poor old state of Mississippi, which is ranked
fiftieth in the United States economically—I was reading in the Jackson paper recently some statistics which
said that Mississippi is not only fiftieth, it's so far behind Arkansas that they say it'll never reach forty-
ninth—but, to continue my thought, I don't think it's
any accident that Mississippi with a population of two
and a half million has produced more fine writers than
the state of Texas, say, with its immense wealth and its
hustling, go-getting entrepreneurial atmosphere, and
its many, many more people.
Jones: Much less Arkansas.
Morris: Exactly.
Jones: At that time did you come to know Larry L.
King and Larry McMurtry and all those Texas writers?
Morris: I didn't get to know Larry King until he was
with *Harper's.* He spent considerable time in Washing-
ton as administrative assistant to a Texas congressman.
I got to know Larry in Washington before I became
editor-in-chief of *Harper's.* I also met McMurtry in
Washington. He was writing books and running a
bookstore. He owns a bookstore in Georgetown. I think
McMurtry's best book is *In a Narrow Grave, Essays on
Texas.* The best writer Texas has produced was
Katherine Anne Porter, who was born and raised there.
She was from Indian Creek, a little west of Austin.
When I was an undergraduate at the University of
Texas Frank Lyell from Jackson, one of Eudora's closest
friends, taught me English—a wonderful teacher, a
literary person in the best sense: he lived for literature.
Katherine Anne Porter was coming in to give a lecture.
Frank Lyell was to meet her at the airport; she was
flying down from Washington or New York. I went

89

with Frank and we met her at the airport and we were heading back toward the university, and she saw the state capitol, a beautiful building, all illuminated against the horizon, and she said, "Frank, do we have time to stop in the capitol for a minute?" We went into the rotunda, and there were tears coming down her face. Frank said, "Katherine Anne, what's wrong?" She said, "My Daddy brought me to this building when I was ten years old, and it was the first real building I ever saw."

Jones: What year did you take over the *Observer*?

Morris: I came back from England and took it over in '60.

Jones: Did you believe in John Kennedy?

Morris: I liked Kennedy. I really did like him. I liked his brother Bobby, too. I never met Jack Kennedy, although I have a number of friends who knew him well, but I did get to know Bobby in New York. Bobby grew tremendously.

Jones: But did your paper support Jack Kennedy?

Morris: Oh, yes, sure. Of course, that's when Lyndon Johnson was making his serious bid for the presidency, in 1960.

Jones: Did you support Johnson?

Morris: Not for the nomination, no. The *Observer* was not representing the liberal wing of the Democratic Party, but we certainly believed in the things that the liberal wing of the party did. Johnson and Sam Rayburn were the adversaries within the party. When Johnson was elected vice-president, I made some gestures to heal the wounds. It didn't work on either side; there were antagonisms between the establishment of the Democratic Party and the liberals that went back many years. I liked Lyndon personally. He was a complex man. That was before the genuine rise of the Republican Party in Texas and the rest of the South. Many of the conservative Democrats were siphoned off by the

Republicans when they started moving. But Lyndon
Johnson was a vital presence in Austin. You'd always
see his big old car zooming around the streets at night,
and you'd see him at the Mexican restaurants and at
Scholz's. He was bigger than life. My friend Bill Brammer, William Brammer, wrote a wonderful political
novel with an unfortunate title: *The Gay Place.* Bill
Brammer, who's now dead, didn't know what "gay"
meant. He was just an old Texas boy. He took the title
from a poem by Scott Fitzgerald, and he wrote a fine
political novel with a character based on Lyndon Johnson. I'm a character in it: Willie England, running a
weekly newspaper in the state capital of the
unidentified largest state in the Southwest. I had just
gotten back from England, and I told Brammer, I said,
"Brammer, at least Thomas Wolfe changed the names
and addresses."

Jones: Lyndon Johnson was the moving force in Texas
politics throughout those years?

Morris: Yes, he was. He and Sam Rayburn. I don't
think Johnson would've ever been elected president had
he not come in the way he did. I don't think the
country was ready for a Southerner as president. Johnson was more of a Southwesterner, I suppose, but he
sure sounded Southern. He was a good president. He
got mired in the tragedy of Vietnam. But some of those
pieces of legislation he got through in the months after
Jack Kennedy was killed . . . .

Jones: The Civil Rights Act of '64 and the others?

Morris: They changed the face of the nation, especially
the South.

Jones: Did you write every day with the *Observer?* Did
you have an editorial in every paper?

Morris: Oh, more than that. We were a weekly, and
I'd write long articles, sometimes ten to fifteen
thousand words. There were never more than two of us
on the paper. But we had some excellent people: Bob

Sherrill, Bill Brammer, Larry Goodwyn, and, of course, Dugger, who was the guiding spirit of the *Observer*, and a number of others. I remember I'd end up every week out at the print shop, the Futura Press on South Congress Street, and stay up all night. We not only had to write everything, we had to make up the paper, proofread, headlines, all of it. I'd set up the typewriter next to the linotype machine and hand in my copy page by page. It was a tough job. I got a lot of nonsense out of my system, I guess. I hope so, having written that many words a week.

Jones: How did you move from a more political scope in your journalism to a more literary or artistic scope as editor of *Harper's*?

Morris: Well, I'd always loved literature. I went to work at *Harper's* as associate editor in 1963. I'm going to have to write a memoir about this. I hope that someday I'll do a sequel to *North Toward Home* called *South Toward Home*. But I want to wait awhile. I want to have a large section in there on New York City and my time at *Harper's*, with all that it symbolizes and represents for me. I joined a staff of several distinguished people who were much older. I think *Harper's* had gotten quite stodgy. I joined the staff with this understanding from John Fischer, whom I did like— he's now dead, too. I disagreed with him on a lot of things. But I did have this understanding that I would take over from him, which I eventually did. I was actually running the magazine without the title of editor for a long time. Jack Fischer would leave the country a great deal. I really wanted to get *Harper's* back to its roots, its traditions. It's the oldest magazine in the country. I wanted to return to its literary traditions by drawing on the best writers. I thought it was going to take a long time, but it didn't. I found it unexpectedly easy. The truly fine writers were ready to have a magazine like that. And I think from the point

of view of the readers, a lot of Americans wanted a
magazine that drew on the best literary traditions of the
United States. And we did it. There was that old con-
tinuing problem with the ownership, you know: who
owns the mimeograph machine? The people who did
own the mimeograph machine were not among the people I respected the most. They didn't know what literature was, or the literary or artistic impulse. So it didn't
last. But things like that don't last in America. They
come and go. And the magazine business itself is in a
condition of flux, getting harder and harder economically—increased printing costs, a damaging policy
on the part of the federal government on postal rates,
and all the rest. Now, in 1980, the magazine business
is in a squeeze, as seen by the decline of the general
interest magazine and the upsurge of the specialized
magazine such as those aimed toward doctors who fly
their own planes and drive blue Mercedeses and like to
ski in Aspen.

Jones: Did you want to leave Texas?

Morris: I was ready to leave. I believe I have in my
concluding pages of *North Toward Home* a description of
my contrasting feelings on Texas and Mississippi. My
feelings for Mississippi were always much more abid-
ing. I learned a lot there in Texas, I got educated there
and still have many good friends there. It just doesn't
have the dark shadows for me that Mississippi does.

Jones: Where were you when John Kennedy was
killed?

Morris: I was out to lunch in New York. I was alone.
It was a Friday, and I returned to the office. Most of the
older editors would take off Friday afternoon and go
home early. I think I was the only male in the office.
All the secretaries started sobbing. One of them said
Kennedy and Johnson had both been killed. But I got
this phone call before they started crying, and it was
from this law professor at Columbia who'd written an

article for *Harper's*. It was going to press. It had some kind of time element on it. It was about Kennedy's appointees to the federal bench. This man called me from Columbia University law school and said, "Have you heard the news? Kennedy and Johnson have both been killed in Dallas." I said, "My God!" And he said, "Well, I hate to tell you this, but I was only calling to see if this was going to have any effect on my article." Evan Thomas, who was a prominent editor at Harper and Row—we shared the same floor with the top editors of the publishing company—came in and said, "We're President Kennedy's publisher and we're going to close down the house today."

Jones: In *North Toward Home*, in your New York section, you write about going to parties given for literary celebrities, and you talk about how alienated you felt at those parties. I wanted to ask you how you came in touch with people you saw at those parties, like Norman Mailer, whose "Prisoner of Sex" you ran.

Morris: We also did Norman's book-length piece that won the Pulitzer Prize, which we called "The Steps of the Pentagon." In his book he changed the title to *Armies of the Night* from the Matthew Arnold poem "Dover Beach." New York City probably seems intimidating to people who've not lived there, but it's really a small world. In the literary and publishing world everybody gets to know everybody else. And I got to know Mailer, eventually quite well. We were friends, and I think we still are. We worked closely together on some of his best work, maybe his very best. You'd run into people at parties. There's an interesting story about how Mailer did this longest magazine article in history: "The Steps of the Pentagon." I remember it was the morning after Houghton Mifflin had given me the big publication party for *North Toward Home*, which would've been in October of '67, in one of those fancy hotels on upper Madison Avenue. They had hundreds of people there, the whole of New York's literary and journalistic establishment, including many of my dear friends: Bill and Rose Styron and Larry King, Dave Halberstam, that group. The next morning I got to my office hung over, and Cass Canfield, who ran Harper and Row, called me on the phone and said, "Norman Mailer's been arrested in Virginia. I hear he's going to do a 10,000-word magazine article on it," this being, of course, during the height of the Vietnam war. So I got on the phone. I couldn't get Mailer, whom I knew, but I got his agent. We talked on the phone all day without even talking to Mailer, and we settled the deal. I think it was 20,000 words for $10,000. And as such things often happen in that strange and intoxicating city, I had to go to the Algonquin Hotel and meet somebody for drinks after work—I think it was the old fellow who wrote the column for the *Commercial Appeal* in Memphis, who had a few bourbons and told me I'd sold out the South—and I was walking up Eighth Avenue toward the subway stop at about six in the afternoon, and who did I run into but Mailer. I said, "Dammit, Norman, we've settled this deal." He said, "I know. I'm gonna write you the finest 20,000 words you've ever had. I'm going to Provincetown tomorrow and start on it, and I'll have it to you one month from today." Well, one month to the day I flew up there in a little plane, and he had 90,000 words. I called up my managing editor Bob Kotlowitz, because we were facing a deadline. And I said, "Bob, we've got 90,000 pretty good words up here." Kotlowitz said, "Great. How many should we run, do you think?" I said, "I think we ought to run them all." He said, "Oh, you do? In three or four installments?" I said, "No, I think we should shoot our wad, run it all at once," and there was this silence on the phone. Longest magazine article in history. But also as a matter of course you'd get to know many of the best writers, such as William Styron, who became one of my dearest friends. I'd actually wanted to meet him, and I knew the only way to meet Bill, whom I'd admired so much through his first novel *Lie Down In Darkness*, was to get him to write for the magazine. So that's how we met. He was working on *The Confessions of Nat Turner.*

Jones: Yes, and he wrote "This Quiet Dust" for you.

Morris: Yes, that's what it was. I put out a special issue of *Harper's* in April of 1965. God, it was a wonderful issue.

Jones: *The South Today.*

Morris: *The South Today: 100 Years After Appomattox.* I wrote Bill in Connecticut and asked him to write a 5,000-word piece on what it was like being a Southerner in the North, you know, all the ironies of that. He said he'd be glad to. The day of the deadline this manuscript came in, and it wasn't 5,000 words, it was 15,000, and it wasn't about a Southerner living in the North, it was about his obsession with slavery and the Nat Turner rebellion. We put the title on it, "This Quiet Dust," from a memorable little poem by Emily Dickinson.

Jones: About going to the old house where Nat committed his first murder?

Morris: Finding the old house. I've subsequently been there. My son David is fast becoming a great photographer. And a writer, too, though he doesn't know it yet. He will, bless him. Several years ago David and I and an old peanut farmer named Dean Waggenback who has a farm right on the North Carolina-Virginia line, which is Nat Turner country, went around with a local historian who showed us everything, all these old houses. David got some memorable pictures of the Whitehead house, where Nat committed his only murder—killed Miss Margaret Whitehead, the belle of the county, with a fencepost. You've got to go up there sometime. Those houses are falling in. They're not close enough to any city where rich people would come out and renovate them and live in them on weekends. They're lying there in decay—the Whitehead house and all the others where this incredible rebellion took place. David got a whole group of distinctive photographs of the houses and the countryside, the brooding peanut country. Good old David was fifteen then. He developed them and mounted them, and we gave them to Bill Styron on his birthday.

Jones: That's something that the house is still there. He wrote that article in '65.

Morris: Yes. And we were there about five years ago, and it was still there. Our peanut farmer friend Dean Waggenback wanted to buy it. He could've bought it for $15,000 with a little land. We were going to do some repairs and engineer a trick on Styron. We were going to have Styron and his wife Rose down and have a little party at the Whitehead house. Actually on that trip my son and my peanut farmer friend and I visited all the battlefields, including, of course, Appomattox, which is a touching place.

Jones: I loved what you wrote in *James Jones: A Friendship* about your visit to Antietam.

Morris: Oh yes. That was Jim Jones and his boy and my boy and me. At that time I was on a stint with the *Washington Star* as guest columnist. That was in '76, our Bicentennial year. I wrote a syndicated column for them three times a week. I don't know why I did that, because I was really out of practice on deadlines. But I'm glad I did it if for no other reason than that trip the four of us took through the Civil War country. Jim Jones died about a year after that.

Jones: I wanted to ask you about the idea behind *The South Today: 100 Years After Appomattox*. Was it your project?

Morris: Yes, I guess so. It's such a hallowed anniversary, and I figured something could be said of some

note on the occasion. It was a very fine magazine issue.
You know, magazine issues don't have long lives,
they're like cotton candy: they taste good but don't last
too long. That's why magazine editors are as a breed
singularly curious people. The ones who don't write
themselves tend to be a little jumpy. So do book editors
who don't write, because they have to exist through
someone else's work. But in capturing a moment a
magazine can be important to the consciousness of a
society. This one particular issue, this *Harper's* issue of
April, 1965, was as fine an issue as any American
magazine in this century.

Jones: How did you get Walker Percy to contribute?

Morris: I didn't know Walker at the time. I was a
great admirer of his, of his first novel *The Moviegoer,*
which I read shortly after it came out in '62. Then
when I was running *Harper's,* I think maybe it was
before I became editor, we ran a sizeable portion of his
book, *The Last Gentleman.* Before that I persuaded Walker to do a piece on "Mississippi: The Fallen Paradise"
for *Harper's.* Later on I got Walker to do a wonderful
piece on New Orleans. And he did some other things
for us. I had a feeling at *Harper's* that you had to
approach the best writers between books when most
writers are in the mood to do something they can see in
print in two or three months. And it worked. It
worked with some of the best writers of our day: Styron, Percy, Mailer, Ellison, and I got the playwright
Arthur Miller to contribute, and you can go right on
down the list, the most courageous and splendid writers
of our day in America. I met Walker—went to visit
him in Covington, Louisiana—and then he came up to
New York once or twice. We had a hangout. At this
time I was living on Long Island. I'd left the city.
When people would come to town—Jim and Gloria
Jones from Europe, or the Styrons from Connecticut,
and others—we'd always stay at the Blackstone Hotel

on Fifty-eighth Street between Park and Madison. It
was inexpensive, and they knew us and were good to
us, knew we were all crazy writers. And they had a
good bar called the Dogwood Room, which we changed
to the Dogpatch. Walker came up to be a judge on the
National Book Awards. He doesn't like New York City
at all. He's like me. I have reservations about Manhattan Island myself. I've even got reservations about
Memphis. Hell, Tupelo's too big. Walker came up,
and I remember bringing him over to the Dogpatch
Room. He hadn't met Styron or Jim Jones or these
people. We took over the whole bar, and my friend
Bobby Van, a restaurateur from Bridgehampton,
started playing the piano. We all ended up at
P. J. Clarke's and closed down the place.

Jones: About what year was this?

Morris: Early '70s: '72, '73.

Jones: Well, *The South Today* came out in hardback.
You were also able to get C. Vann Woodward to contribute.

Morris: Vann Woodward, Louis Rubin, Jonathan
Daniels, and did we have Ralph Ellison in there?

Jones: No.

Morris: Well, I subsequently got to know Ralph Ellison quite well. Ellison and I came to Jackson once. We
gave a joint lecture at Millsaps.

Jones: What year was that?

Morris: I think this would have been '69 or '70. We
brought the young son of the president of Random
House down who was a student at Brown University
and was thinking about doing an exchange program at
Tougaloo. This Yankee kid, his eyes were opened when
he came to Mississippi.

Jones: Ellison had a tough time at Tougaloo in '68
when he was shouted down by the militants for his
commitment to being an artist first and then a black.

Morris: Was that in '68?

Jones: '68.

Morris: Well, that was not the same visit. We came down together later. Ellison always fought for the artistic imagination. *Invisible Man* is one of the towering novels of American literature.

Jones: Let me ask you this: during the time when you were with the *Observer* and then beginning with *Harper's*, the civil rights movement was ripping the Mississippi of your boyhood apart at the seams and changing the lives of everyone who was here during those years. How did that affect you or your art?

Morris: You're talking about the early '60s?

Jones: Yes.

Morris: The height of it?

Jones: Right. All the violence of '63, '64, '65.

Morris: Well, you see, I witnessed that from afar on the television screen in New York City.

Jones: How did it make you feel?

Morris: It affected me profoundly, as I suppose it would any civilized Southerner or American. I was torn up by it, literally torn up piece by piece. But, of course, I was not here during the middle of it. Witnessing from afar those events on one's home ground was a devastating experience for me. I later got to know many of the people involved. I was in Austin, Texas, when the James Meredith event hit this campus.

Jones: One hundred yards away.

Morris: Right up the road. I almost came over. It's been eighteen years, and, of course, the changes that have taken place all around us here on this campus are interesting to observe. I often wonder what William Faulkner would think going over to the Ole Miss Coliseum and seeing sixty percent of the Ole Miss basketball team black. He would've gone to watch, too.

Jones: Yes. That's really part of what I was asking. As a Mississippi writer who grew up before this happened, how the changes in the very fiber of the state of Mississippi brought on by the movement changed the way you approached your art that is so deeply rooted in place.

Morris: Yes. Well, let me make another point first. I always had a strong feeling that grew in me more and more in the late '60s that the important thing for the Deep South, and especially Mississippi, that was both symbolic and substantial, was the massive integration of the public schools. When that came in 1970 I wrote a little book about it called *Yazoo.* I had to come back to see that. I was in charge of a national magazine at the time, and I had to be far away from the office to do it. I wish I'd have had another four or five months on that book. I couldn't take the time; I was running a magazine. Once that happened, even given all the shortcomings of it, and the private academies and the failures and everything, it ushered in a whole new period. It took a lot of pressure off of people, including white people, in the Deep South. Mississippi is not the tense place it was, you know, the wrought-up, tense place obsessed with one issue: race, which it was. This has all taken place in the last ten or twelve years. Not to say that this is a paradise, but, hell, nothing under the Lord's sun is paradise.

Jones: Do you think the civil rights movement will have an effect on Mississippi's tradition of spawning many great writers, the home of Faulkner and Miss Welty and the whole list? Do you think the unquestionableness of the race question for so many years is what perhaps created that climate?

Morris: No, it's part of a much larger fabric, and the larger fabric is that of a basically communal society with a storytelling tradition, with blacks living among us so close giving it its flamboyance and color, so to speak, and its guilt, and its substance. The more sizeable question in future years for Mississippi and Mississippi writers and Southern writers is, can this kind of

heritage continue to elicit good writing. I don't want to
see the suburbs of Memphis get down here as far as
Yoknapatawpha County. I don't want to see the New
South in Holly Springs. I have mixed feelings about the
New South. You can get off at the Atlanta airport, that
whole modern cosmos, and you *still* know you're in the
South. Yet I feel in my soul that Southern writing will
endure.

Jones: You know, I'm just beginning to read the kind
of book you've probably read a hundred times, that's
trying to explain the great outpouring of Southern writing from '25 to '55. Some people say it's the race
question in Mississippi and the Deep South, and the
fact that it was intractable. Other people say it's a
question of coming to grips with history, setting history, the difficult history of the South, to rest. Others
say it's the problem of the Southern family romance. I
don't know.

Morris: Well, which came first, John, the chicken or
the egg, to use the terrible cliché. It's all a part of it. I
remember the first question I got on my final examina-
tions at Oxford University, which lasted about six
hours a day for two weeks; it just so happened that my
first essay question covered that period from 1850 to
1861 in American history, which haunted me for a
year. They'd give you twenty questions on each of many
papers, and you were required to answer, I think, four
essay questions, so you had a choice. You had to dress
up in an awful stiff white shirt with a tie and a blue
suit and a gown and mortarboard, and they wouldn't
let you smoke in this big Victorian examination hall in
Oxford. I was chewing bubble gum, and these Englishmen around me accused me of making them do
poorly because of my bubble gum. I even brought in
some chewing tobacco to the examination hall at Oxford University; first time I'd chewed tobacco since my
baseball-playing days back in the Mississippi Delta. It

was even "Brown Mule," which I'd bought at the PX of
an American air base. I brought a little paper cup and
was writing these history questions and spitting. These
Englishmen didn't like that either. But the first question was: "Was the American Civil War fought over the
black man?" And I looked at that question and said,
"Oh, Goddammit." And then I never even finished it. I
wrote the whole three hours on that single question. I
think I got the equivalent of an A+ on it, even though
I only wrote on this one question. So what's the answer? The blacks, by their very presence, the whole
history of the institution of slavery, made the South
different. One of the impulses to the truly distinguished Southern fiction over the years has derived from
differentness; the fact that the South was both a part of
the broader American civilization, and removed from
it. And it still is removed from it, even though up here
on Sorority Row last month in November of 1980 all
you saw were Reagan stickers. The South still is somewhat removed from it. And the Ole Miss coeds, whom
I call "goldfish," are certainly different. You know why
I call them "goldfish"?

Jones: Why?

Morris: If you've ever watched goldfish in a bowl, they
love for you to look at them, they dart around a lot,
they don't think too much, and they don't like to be
still for too very long, and then when you put your
hand down in the bowl to touch one of them they swim
away furiously. Oh, well—just an observation.

Jones: That's it. I did a really interesting interview
with Evans Harrington up here about the changes that
have come about since Meredith, and he said the Ole
Miss coed today is no different from the Ole Miss coed
of 1961; it's just that being polite to blacks is part of
her repertoire now, whereas she'd always been polite to
rednecks.

Morris: Evans and I've talked about that, and I think

there's truth to it. They're polite now the way they used to be to the Snopeses. It's fascinating, the ironies you see here. I'm really intrigued with Ole Miss. I love the place. A state university is supposed to be a reflection of the state that nurtures it. The greatness of Ole Miss lies in places other than the classroom. The ironies that you observe here! I was sitting one afternoon in the bleachers of the baseball field. Sometimes I'd go over there last spring in the sunshine and grade my papers and watch my friend Jake Gibbs, the Ole Miss coach, and his squad work out. There were these four black Ole Miss basketball players whom I recognized from the games—the season was over and they were going to the gym to jog or something—being led by Sean Tuohy, the white, playmaking guard from New Orleans. "Now boys, now come on, let's go. Come on!" There was an interesting moment at the Ole Miss-Mississippi State football game. Were you there in the rain?

Jones: Yes, in the end zone.

Morris: Yes, a couple of weeks ago. There was a moment that was actually more important than the game. A black male cheerleader, the first Ole Miss black male cheerleader, who's a freshman now—they unveil their freshman cheerleaders the last game of the season—holding up the white coed cheerleader. I hear he got some shouts, too. He works for my friend William Lewis who owns Neilson's, and the kid told William that he got some taunts, people yelled at him and the white girl.

Jones: Have you ever read the poem by a college professor, "To Aphrodite On Your Leaving"?

Morris: No. Is it about the Ole Miss coeds?

Jones: It's about coeds in general.

Morris: Did you ever read Terry Southern's classic piece in *Esquire* about the Ole Miss baton twirling clinic?

Jones: No.

Morris: Look that up sometime.

Jones: To return to what we were talking about earlier. Here you were in New York City running a magazine that I'm sure was running you crazy; how did you ever find time to sit down and write up *North Toward Home?*

Morris: I took a leave of absence for several months. I remember I had to go to the bank and borrow money because I wasn't getting paid by *Harper's.* I had a certain amount of it already written. This would've been in 1966. There was a wonderful editor with Houghton Mifflin in Boston, Dorothy De Santillana. We started corresponding back when I was with the *Texas Observer.* She wanted me to do a book. They had and still have the most distinguished prize for first books, called the Houghton Mifflin Literary Fellowship.

Jones: Which *North Toward Home* won.

Morris: That's right. They've given it to some good people: Robert Penn Warren, Philip Roth, Bill Brammer, a lot of people.

Jones: Ellen Douglas, who's teaching here this semester, won one.

Morris: I think Elizabeth Spencer got one also. Dorothy wanted me to apply for that. I got it on the basis of an outline. But I remember I wrote the bulk of *North Toward Home* in an apartment we had on West End Avenue and Ninety-fourth Street. I wrote a good part of it on a big table in the kitchen. I think I wrote the first draft of the Mississippi part in about three weeks. I later had to go back and do a lot of work on it, of course. I do remember that my leave of absence ended, and Jack Fischer and others wanted me to come back to work, and I hadn't written my New York section. So I'd do that on weekends and at night. We bought an old farmhouse north of New York around Brewster. I'd go out there and work on it.

Jones: And ride the commuter train.

Morris: I did that one summer with an Ole Miss man named Bob Childres, whom I'd known at the other Oxford, now also dead. Everybody seems to be dead these days. Childres and I were close friends, and our wives were close, so we bought a farmhouse up where they had a place sixty miles north of Manhattan. Bob Childres and I commuted all summer, the summer of '66, I think. By the end of the summer we were wrecks. We'd try to meet for the 4:29 Express for Brewster in Grand Central Station. We'd always meet in the bar car. The last day of that hot terrible summer—it was two hours each way—we sat down and ordered two big gin and tonics, and as I recall Childres had to wear a bowler hat. He was practicing law at Thomas E. Dewey's. We didn't say anything for about five minutes and the train pulled out, and finally Childres turned around and said, "Goddammit, Morris, what are two old Mississippi boys doing up here commuting, being commuters?" But *North Toward Home*—it struck a strange chord somewhere, and not just in the South. I got literally thousands of letters from all over the country. I think one of the reasons I got so many was that I was accessible when the book came out; you know, I was at *Harper's* and had a mailing address. I don't know what it was.

Jones: Everyone I know has read it.

Morris: Well, I've had that experience too; everybody's read the thing. Of course, I guess that's what writing's for.

Jones: Where did the impulse come from to sit down and write up your memoirs at thirty?

Morris: I don't know. I had a lot to say. I had stories I wanted to tell. That's where the impulse comes from: your memory. Writing is memory, the burden of memory. It's a big burden. You exorcise the demons.

Jones: Was there any autobiography that you read dur-

ing that period that gave you special inspiration, such
as *Lanterns on the Levee?*
Morris: Of course I read *Lanterns on the Levee.* I'll tell
you one that really did impress me: it was an early book
by Mark Twain called *Roughing It.*
Jones: Yes, about his experiences gold mining and
such.
Morris: Yes, going out to the West. The first half of
that book is one of the best memoirs in American literature. It falls apart in the end for some reason. But that
book summoned me, as if Mark Twain were whispering
something private to me, just between the two of us,
saying: "Hey, kid, do it." Autobiographical writing is a
sturdy strain in American letters. *The Autobiography of
Lincoln Steffens*, I remember I loved that. *Lanterns on the
Levee* is a fascinating book. *A Moveable Feast* by
Hemingway.
Jones: Cruel book.
Morris: It was a cruel book, a posthumous book. A lot
of posthumous books are cruel.
Jones: Tell me how sitting down and writing
nonfiction differs from writing fiction.
Morris: It's easier. Fiction has to have a flow to it over
a long period of time. Nonfiction is quite different, of
course, and easier. The patterns are more systematic.
Jones: You were saying that there were parts of *North
Toward Home* that you would change today if you could.
Morris: Well, anything you look back on that you've
written years ago, your natural impulse is to improve
the language. I guess you get better as you get older, I
don't know. You certainly accumulate more experience,
which should have wisdom inherent in it, and writing
is an expression of everything you know. But in putting
out some of these nonfiction pieces of mine that Larry
Wells is publishing next spring, I've come across things
that I'd forgotten I'd ever written. That's a funny feeling. I had to go back and reread some parts of *North*

Toward Home and *Yazoo*, and even my memoir of Jim
Jones, that I'd forgotten I'd written. Especially parts of
North Toward Home. I think my first feeling was: "Hey,
this is pretty good." But not having read any of it since
you wrote it is an exceedingly strange feeling. Of course
you have a temptation to change your hard-earned
words, but you have to go with what you were at a
given moment, what you were thinking about, what
you were obsessed with, who you really were. You can't
tamper with yourself. You have to grow with your own
work.

Pete's getting on this tape, barking at the kids out
on Faculty Row. This may mystify some ascetic scholar
of the year 2075. He's the best dog in the world. He'd
come to my classes at Ole Miss last spring. One day I
thought I was being quite intelligent on something
that had to do with American fiction, and Pete, my dog
and brother, was up on the top row of the lecture hall
lying down next to my friend Dean Faulkner Wells,
and in the middle of the sentence I was coming out
with I heard this gasping yawn that reverberated
through the lecture hall, and I thought, "Oh, my God,
I'm just putting them to sleep." It was my dog Pete
yawning. He'd heard it all before. When my friend
Pete dies, I die.

Jones: Did your experience at *Harper's* sour you on
journalism?

Morris: No, it didn't sour me. I was unhappy for a
while. I missed the perquisites of high station. I missed
my two secretaries, one Jewish, one black, and the
"appurtenances of power," in quotes, like Manhattan
expense accounts. But it didn't sour me on journalism
or magazines. It buttressed certain things I'd always
felt: never put too much trust in rich people, especially
rich Yankee Wasps.

Jones: You've had first-hand experience with real re-
pression of a type that few people in this country expe-

rience. At the *Daily Texan* you were censured as an
undergraduate editor. At *Harper's* you were in conflict
with the people who represented the money behind the
magazine, and you resigned over the mention of censor-
ship. I was wondering how that affected your sensibilities.

Morris: I ain't bitter, just reflective. Any time you get
close to the heart of things, to the source of human
things, you're going to run into this trouble, especially
when you have a reckless regard for the things that you
have to hold up. As my friend James Dickey would say,
sometimes a man has to be reckless in behalf of the
qualities he cares for passionately. And say, what the
hell? This is a democratic society where the First
Amendment works most of the time. I guess the ideal
situation at an institution like *Harper's* in those years
was to have owned the mimeograph machine yourself.
But it takes money to own the mimeograph machine.
Of course money controls; on a national scale, the
young editor must find the right money. It's hard. It's
draining to deal with rich owners, especially when you
don't talk the same language about your own civilization. Putting those years at *Harper's* in their context, I
do think we said something about the America of that
day, the exacerbated mood of the country during the
Vietnam years, and I do think we tried to stand for
something civilized. We had a good magazine, maybe
the best of our generation. But, as I say, these things
come and go.

Jones: Where did you get the idea for *Yazoo?*

Morris: I saw a little piece in the *New York Times.* This
federal court order had come out of New Orleans in
December '69, and it caught my eye, buried on a back
page. This was, of course, sixteen years after Brown vs.
Board of Education of 1954. The South had fought this
through the thickets of the law for sixteen years, but
the federal court order out of New Orleans was it. I

wanted to be down at home to see and to observe the consequences. I'm glad I did. It was a fascinating moment. It was sad, and funny, as most important moments are.

Jones: You certainly froze it in time.

Morris: I think the book was fair enough. Historians are going to have to use it. I just wish I'd had maybe four more months, which I simply couldn't take due to the circumstances of my profession at the time. But I'm pleased with it. It's in a way a continuation of *North Toward Home.*

Jones: Was it in *North Toward Home* or *Yazoo* when you talk about going to the Citizens' Council meeting?

Morris: That was in the first book. That would've been in the summer of 1955. They had an organizing meeting of the Citizens' Council in Yazoo City then.

Jones: After seeing that kind of recalcitrance, did you think by 1970 that desegregation could come about peacefully?

Morris: No. Quite the contrary, I saw violence in the future. What did big Hodding Carter call the Citizens' Council? The Ku Klux Klan with a clipped moustache. It was the establishment. Eventually the courts had to win out.

Jones: I've been doing a project on the civil rights movement in Mississippi, and I've always been amazed how over just five years from the violence and bloodshed of 1964 there could've been a turnabout in Mississippi. I would've thought the old segregationists would have to die out before it could be done peacefully. But it is remarkable that in five years, an incredibly short period of time in terms of history, this could have happened.

Morris: It really is. I think it had something to do with having no more choices. Once the inevitable arrived, the Deep South by and large responded very well. It responded from its finer instincts—as Abraham

Lincoln said in his inaugural, "the better angels of our nature." It's one of the most interesting things to watch, the ramifications of the things you see, like Sean Tuohy and the black basketball players, and the black cheerleader. Cleve Donald was the second black to attend Ole Miss after Meredith, and he's been my neighbor across the street over here on Faculty Row. He's on a leave of absence in Washington now. Cleve and I have had some pretty good talks drinking beer here or at his house.

Jones: He's an interesting man.

Morris: Yes, I like Cleve. I miss him.

Jones: He was deeply involved with Medgar Evers down in Jackson.

Morris: Yes, that's right. I hope he's doing a book on Medgar Evers. He's done a fine essay on Evers. The University Press of Mississippi has done a book called *Mississippi Heroes*, which Dean Faulkner Wells edited and asked me to do a little introduction to. That essay is included.

Jones: You know in your book *Yazoo* you talk about Melvin Leventhal and meeting him, an NAACP attorney, and his wife Alice Walker in Jackson. Mel Leventhal wrote a criticism of *Yazoo* where he said you were only interested in desegregation in terms of the white community.

Morris: That was at a congressional hearing, wasn't it?

Jones: I don't know.

Morris: I think it was. Maybe Mel Leventhal had to say that. Hell, he was protecting his political flanks. Don't blame him. The book itself may last longer than Mel Leventhal. I believe he did say that my main interest was the white community. Well, I'm white, and I suppose that bias was inevitable. I'll stand by the book. I think I was basically right in that book. *Yazoo* is two throws away from being a classic, even if I say it myself. I'm always surprised that there's been so little

good nonfiction on this subject. Surprisingly little—
Marshall Frady's done some good things on this. I made
some presumptions at the time that I'm not too sure
about now. I think I underestimated the efficacy and
the durability of the white private academies. That was
probably the biggest flaw in that book. That and the
durability of great poverty on any kind of civilizing
change.

Jones: I think everybody was saying at the time that
no one could afford to send their three or four kids to
private schools from grades one through twelve, not in
Mississippi.

Morris: Yes, I thought so.

Jones: But I've always been amazed at how accurate
you've been in your presumptions and predictions, not
only in *Yazoo.* I saw an interview done with you in June
of '73, fully a year before Richard Nixon's resignation,
where you said impeachment is a nineteenth century
procedure and that there's no way our system could
stand it, but that the president would effectively be
rendered of his power to the point where he'd have to
resign.

Morris: Did I say that?

Jones: Yes. You predicted the outcome of Watergate
precisely, fully a year before it ended with Nixon's
resignation.

Morris: Where was I when I said that?

Jones: On the ETV "A Conversation With" series with
Howard Lett, when you were talking about *The Last of
the Southern Girls.*

Morris: Oh, that's right. I remember that, down in
Jackson.

Jones: You did. And you were one of the first people I
ever read that said that Mississippi would be the land
where racial reconciliation, in whatever form it was
going to take, would occur.

Morris: Yes, I think I was the first person who said
that, and some people criticized it then.

Jones: I think it's true.

Morris: I do too. There's a long way to go, though. Of course, the person who really understood this so well in his generation was Faulkner. There's no more revealing a story—it's one of my favorite short stories—"Delta Autumn." You know, the story about Uncle Ike McCaslin's last hunt, and the mulatto woman who comes with the baby to the hunting camp. There's a resonance in that story. Mr. Bill knew what he was talking about. And of course the Northern liberals gave him hell. There's a word called *prescience*.

Jones: It's in Percy's book, *The Last Gentleman*, on every other page: "the prescient engineer."

Morris: Yes, some people don't like prescience.

Jones: Do you still believe in desegregation?

Morris: I'll tell you what I do believe in strongly is *access*, having access to the institutions, the public institutions. Desegregation may not be working terribly well in Mississippi right now, or on the Ole Miss campus. You know the two institutions in Oxford where desegregation is working the best? The athletic department at Ole Miss and the bar at the Holiday Inn. Have you ever been in the bar of the Holiday Inn with Clyde Goosby, the black bartender?

Jones: Yes, I went there in college.

Morris: The schools in a democratic society had to be desegregated, had to be open to blacks. Even if there are places that are 90 percent black, and there are schools out in Yazoo County that are 90 percent black.

Jones: Hell, in Jackson.

Morris: In Jackson and various places, the public institutions are open to them. That's coming a long way. And it happened ten years ago. The Northern liberals laughed at William Faulkner in the late '40s in an interview he had with *Reporter* magazine, and he later claimed he was drunk when he gave the interview. They asked him what he thought was the future of race relations in the South, desegregation and all that, and he replied that it's not going to be so much a matter down here of whether the whites want it, it's going to be a matter of whether the blacks want it. And, of course, the Northern liberals laughed at him and called him an old Mississippi fool. He was right. Maybe the blacks don't want it, but at least given the great sweep of history, let's give them the choice. If they don't want it, fine. Mississippi is about the only state in America that cares about all this anyway. Even the old conservatives are somewhat bemused. Why not? It's an interesting society. Even the old racists are fascinating. All this crazy stuff is an expression of why Mississippi is the most interesting state in the Union. This is a funny time here, and very touching. Let's keep our eyes open and not forget how to laugh and cry, maybe at the same time. At least we care. Who gives a damn but crazy old Mississippi? Who cares in Wilkes-Barre?

Jones: Mr. Faulkner said, "The whites have already lost their heads. It's now up to the blacks whether they'll keep theirs."

Morris: He knew what he was talking about, Mr. Bill.

Jones: Are you very distressed at the attacks on busing and school desegregation with the new conservative tide? In *Yazoo* you manifested a strong belief in the possibilities of desegregation in Mississippi. Do you still believe in those possibilities?

Morris: Yes, I do, I suppose. As I say, I think a lot of it will depend on the black attitude. You know, it's still so early. I hear stories all the time about the friendship between white and black kids here at Oxford High School: white and black kids playing sports together, going to parties. This is bound, over the long stretch, to have an effect on the next generation and the generation after that. It's up to them, what they want here. After all, we're talking about civilization, which is the hardest, most precarious thing in the world, people trying to be kind to each other, reasonably tolerable. And this is a biracial society, by God, or the closest America has to one. Good for it! Human beings tend, of course, by our nature to be so much the creatures of our own time, of our own generation. That's also part of being human. We're creatures of our own moment. I've always been a student of history, and I don't believe in the inevitability of anything. I don't have too many set theories about history, except that history goes on. It does that. It goes on and on.

Jones: Let me ask you this: you had always been a man of social convictions and worked with social concerns in your days with the *Observer* and *Harper's*. Was it hard to put that all aside when you sat down to write *The Last of the Southern Girls?*

Morris: Not really. I guess it's a matter of one's role. I had this notion when I went to work for *Harper's* that a man could be both an editor and a writer. I think I got this idea from the nineteenth century. I thought I could be like William Dean Howells, you know, who was editor of both the *Atlantic* and *Harper's*, and a writer. I was wrong. In the nineteenth century, among other things, they didn't have telephones. You can become the victim of telephones. That's why I hate talking on the phone. Sometimes I put it in the refrigerator. It's because of my days on *Harper's*. I'd go out to the men's room and come back and there'd be eight messages, none of which mattered; but it didn't take me very long to be disabused of that idea of the dual role. You can't be both a magazine editor and a writer. The functions of the two, far from supplementing each other, are mutually antagonistic for me. It was good for me to get out, to be on my own and not be the editor anymore. It's a young man's profession, being an editor.

Jones: Really?

Morris: I've seen too many people get old in that profession, or too ideological, or too spoiled by one's self-importance. An editor ain't really all that important, when you get right down to it. You really are an expression of other people. You live through other people's work. And if you're a writer, no one's going to help you. You're on your own with no one to help you. This has both its rewards and its hazards. It's lonesome. You get scared to death sometimes. Especially when you're between books and the money's not coming in and you're paying $15,000 a year tuition, or $12,000 up at Amherst, Massachusetts, and your agent hasn't sold your latest magazine piece quite yet. You've got to keep your dog in Alpo. Right, Pete? But the rewards are the rewards of being your own person. I'd rather sleep till noon than commute on a train every day. So I guess looking back on it I was probably ready to leave. I missed it for a while. The question of the social role, being political and everything, I've never really dwelt on that too much. I don't miss that activist role at all. At *Harper's* we weren't directly political, of course. As for writing, I believe in it, and I've some good books in me before I hang my saddle on the wall.

Jones: Certainly. May I ask you just a few more questions?

Morris: Sure.

Jones: Would you have fought for the South in the Civil War?

Morris: I've thought about that. I guess I would've. So would Foote and Whitehead and Hannah and Percy— and in fact all the present-day Percys of Mississippi. Shelby's already served twenty years of labor on his *Civil War.* He knows the passion and blood. Hell, so does Walker. So does Eudora. That war is the thread which runs through us as a civilization. You've got to understand that war, all of it, to understand America— the greatness and sadness of America. Our tragedy and promise and redemption. I'd have opposed that war, just as Shelby and Walker and Eudora would've. But when it happened, we'd have been with the South.

How could we not? Shelby would've got it at Shiloh,
which is fitting, Barry at Corinth, Whitehead at Iuka,
Walker at Spotsylvania. With luck I'd have lasted till
Petersburg. Eudora, our nurse in the hospitals,
would've survived us and written some words about
it—sad words, but some ironic and funny ones too,
great words—remembrance, which she does anyway.
We'd have been fighting over a lot more than slavery.
As Faulkner said, the love of the land mattered most,
all that. Sure, I'd have fought and died, though with
some considerable reluctance. Wouldn't you? Time has
dealt with us here.

Jones: Will you go on writing?

Morris: I don't know what else to do. I hate wearing a
shirt and tie. They make my neck itch. I really do like
to sleep till noon. I loathe committee meetings. I like
taking a leak outdoors. I can't tolerate office hours. I
can't suffer the organized fools. I like sitting down on
an afternoon and dwelling upon the things I care about,
or remember with feeling, and then trying to give a
little sense to them. Moments of passion remembered
in times of tranquility, Henry James said.

Jones: So words give you strength?

Morris: Well, again, I don't have an alternative. I
have no alternative to words. I guess they're better than
sex. They last, though sex and words are good together.

Jones: If your great-grandson and great-granddaughter
came into these State Archives in Jackson, Mississippi,
many years from now to read these words transcribed
from this tape, is there anything you'd add for their
eyes?

Morris: I'd certainly like my great-grandson or
-daughter to read them. I'd want my great-grandson or
great-granddaughter to know that I love and care for
them deep in my heart, even though I'll never know
them. I'd want them to know they're on my mind. I'd
want them to feel that human life, at its best, is a cycle

of love. I'd want them to care passionately for the presence of the past—you know, the little moments and the big historic ones. I'd like them to go to the cemeteries in Yazoo City and Raymond. I'd like them to care about their fellow human beings, maybe in an Old Testament sense—that we're all in it together, and all in for a tough time. They'll learn soon enough that to live is to suffer, that there are places in our hearts in which suffering must enter. I'd like them to care passionately, however, for the fine moments of life—all of them—and to savor life's immemorial delights, and to not let much guilt and shame get them down.

Jones: And what would you tell them about death?

Morris: Oh, to hell with death. I'd say, "My children, continue the Mississippi-American line. Care for Western civilization." Death's not all it's made out to be. Death is overrated. The poet Marvell said, "Had we both world enough and time." We don't get either, the world or the time, but if we care, we'll leave our reminder: we were here, and we were part of it.

Photograph Courtesy of Mississippi Educational Television Network

Margaret Walker Alexander

March 13, 1982

She lives in a house at the end of Margaret Walker Alexander Drive in Jackson. Earlier on the day I came to call she'd attended a neighbor's wedding, and when the squad of young children who met me at the door brought me into the den to meet her, she was resting on the couch. She apologized, got to her feet and shooed away the kids, and suggested that we move to her study for the interview. As soon as I set up my equipment among her books, scattered papers and memorabilia, we began. She does not appear to be a woman in her seventies. There is nothing frail about her. It quickly became clear that ideas are her stimulant. When the issues we were discussing reached some level of complexity, she became animated. I realized in talking with her that, although she has behind her a distinguished literary career reaching back to the 1930s, her work is not done. She knows too many of the questions about black American experience to stop attempting to find answers in her work.

Jones: What I wanted to do, Dr. Alexander, to begin with, is just ask you to give me something about your early background and your early education, something

about your parents, where they were from, and things
of that nature.

Alexander: I was born two hundred fifty miles from
here in Birmingham, Alabama, and I grew up two
hundred miles from here, southwest of Jackson, in New
Orleans, Louisiana. My father was born in the West
Indies. He came from Jamaica Buff Bay, Jamaica, British West Indies. At the time it was a British possession. He came to this country about seventy-four years
ago, in 1908. He came to study and to become a minister, a Methodist minister. He went for a while to Tuskegee Institute, where Booker T. Washington and
George Washington Carver and Emmett J. Scott were
at the time. He did not like Tuskegee. It was not the
school that he wanted to go to and that he thought
about; and a friend of his came there and told him that
where he wanted to go was Atlanta. He left Tuskegee
and in 1910 he entered the divinity school called Gammon Theological Seminary in Atlanta. He graduated in
1913, and even before he had taken his degree he was
selected to be an interim supply pastor in Pensacola,
Florida. On the way there he met my maternal grandmother on the train, and she told him that her daughter played for the church where he was going. Her
daughter was her oldest child, and my aunt. My
mother was away in school at the time, in Washington,
and when she came home that summer, my father saw
her for the first time and fell in love at first sight. They
were married the next year; and the night they were
married they went to Birmingham, Alabama, where my
father pastored the Second Church, as they called it
then, in Enon Ridge, where all four of their children
were born. I'm the oldest of four, and I was born in
Birmingham—possibly, I guess, the next year after
they were married. My sister is almost two years
younger, and then another sister is two years younger
than she; and we have a brother. The four of us are still
alive and kicking, I guess. All of us teach school, at

least I did until I retired. My two sisters teach. My
mother is a music teacher—at least she taught music
for twenty years—is now, of course, retired and almost
bedridden. She's well up in age, still lives in New
Orleans in the house where my father put us when we
moved there in 1925. Two weeks after we went to New
Orleans we moved into this house, where my family
still lives. It's uptown in the University section of New
Orleans, in walking distance from Tulane and Loyola
and Newcomb, five blocks from the school on St.
Charles Avenue where my mother and father taught,
which later became Dillard University. I grew up in a
home surrounded by books and music. As you can see,
I like books.

Jones: You're surrounded by books here.

Alexander: Yes, my father's books were his most
prized possession; and he had a room full of books. My
mother had a very good piano. At the time it didn't
seem like much, but now, looking back, they realize it
was a very good piano. They began housekeeping with
books and a piano. A typewriter and their books and
the piano were all their worldly possessions, besides
their clothes. They had no furniture. At first they
rented a room, when they were first married, to live in.
I was born not in a parsonage, but in one of those
rented places, the old Boulware house, where they lived
when they first lived in Birmingham; but by the time I
was six years old, my father had bought a house in
Birmingham. We went to New Orleans when I was
ten, and he bought another house. So I have grown up
under the roof that my parents owned. It's always been
a feeling of pride that I can't remember when we
rented.

Jones: Yes, ma'am.

Alexander: I think that's typical of a certain type of
people in the South, always feeling that you should
have your own house and land.

Jones: Yes, right.

Alexander: It goes as far back as the first years after slavery when my great-grandmother, who's in *Jubilee*, sought and succeeded finally in getting a home of her own.

Jones: I remember.

Alexander: It's part of a Southern tradition, I think. I went to school first here in Mississippi. My very first day of school was in Meridian, Mississippi. My father and mother were teaching that year in a church school in Meridian called Haven. They stayed there the year that I was five years old; then they moved back to Birmingham. And when they moved back to Birmingham, I went to public school for a while, oh, two or three years. The school where they were teaching in Birmingham burned, and that's the reason my father sought employment in New Orleans. He taught for a while there in the public schools, taught at Miles College and at the public high school, which was known then as Industrial High and became later Parker High. In New Orleans, I attended the Model grade school, which was part of the old New Orleans University where my parents were working. My father taught Bible and philosophy, religion and philosophy; and my mother taught music. My two sisters and my brother are all musical. I wish I were! I always wanted to play the piano—I took some lessons—I tried to learn to play the violin, and I tried to learn to sing, but I am literally tone-deaf and can't even pitch myself on key. I think those are the important things about my early education. I finished grade school and high school in New Orleans. I went to Gilbert Academy, and I had two years of college in a black college where my mother and father were teaching, before I transferred to Northwestern in Evanston, Illinois. I was seventeen when I went there, and I was a junior in college. It seems as if I might have been precocious; maybe I was just pushed along, because I went to school when I was four or five

124

years old. I could read when I was four. I finished grade
school when I was eleven, and I finished high school
when I was fourteen—in three years I finished high
school; and I would have finished college at eighteen,
but I was out my senior year because we had no money
to send me back to Northwestern, and I was a nervous
wreck anyway! But I went back following my
nineteenth birthday, and I graduated that next summer. I was nineteen as a senior, but about six weeks
after my twentieth birthday I graduated from Northwestern. I started working seven months later on the
WPA writers' project in Chicago. It was a wonderful
place to work, because many very famous and illustri-
ous writers were on that project. Some of them I knew.
Richard Wright was on that project. Nelson Algren
was on that project. James Farrell's wife was there when
I went there; I don't know that James Farrell ever really
was on the project, but he was around, and he had
written his Studs Lonigan stories then.
Jones: Right!
Alexander: Arna Bontemps was a special person on
that project. Katherine Dunham, the dancer, was on
that project. John T. Frederick, who was editor of the
Midland Magazine, was project director for a while. It
started with Louis Worth, who was a professor in
sociology from University of Chicago and before I had
gotten on it, I had worked for the Institute for Juvenile
Research, which was directed by Clifford Shaw; and he
had two men under him who went on to fame in the
area of sociology—Eustace Hayden, Jr., and Joseph
Lohmann, who went out to California and became
sheriff of Orange County. The people on that project
were just amazing. Willard Motley and Frank Yerby
were on that project, and Fenton Johnson. They tell me
Studs Terkel was there. I vaguely remember Studs Terkel, but I don't think that I remember him from the
project. And Saul Bellow had been at Northwestern

with the same teacher in creative writing that I had, but he graduated two years later, so that if he came on the project I didn't know him.

Jones: Now, who was the teacher?

Alexander: The teacher was Edward Buell Hungerford, a wonderful scholar, and great man. I think there's a card right there on the desk from him just recently.

Jones: There it is.

Alexander: He was my favorite teacher; he's up in age now.

Jones: That's right. Let me reach back. We've covered a lot of ground, so let me reach back and set up something here. You say your father was at Tuskegee before you were born? You were born in 1915?

Alexander: Yes. My father was at Tuskegee around 1908. Booker T. Washington died, I think, the year I was born. It's interesting, because Frederick Douglass died the year my mother was born; and my mother remembered hearing and reading of Paul Laurence Dunbar, but he was dead about nine or ten years before I was born.

Jones: That's what I was wondering, because you said your father didn't like Tuskegee, and I was wondering if it was . . .

Alexander: He didn't want that kind of education. My father said that when he went to Tuskegee, they put him in the kitchen washing dishes, and he broke all the dishes. Then they put him in the fields, and he was no good there. So they said, "What can you do? What do you know how to do?" Everybody at Tuskegee worked. And he said, "Well, I keep books and I can take shorthand and I type." "Oh," they said, "you belong in the office." So he went into Emmett J. Scott's office, who was assistant to Booker T. Washington at the time, and my father worked there until he left Tuskegee. But he said it was a school basically for

vocational and industrial education; and even though
Tuskegee became in a way a great university, it did not
emphasize classical education.

Jones: Right.

Alexander: That's right; and my father wanted to
study for the ministry, which was a professional,
graduate type of education. He had already completed
what was the equivalent of college work before he came
over. He did later take a degree from a college in this
country. He got his divinity degree at Gammon and
then went to Northwestern and took a master's in Biblical literature. After that, my mother could not per-
suade him to go further. He said he didn't have any use
for a doctorate and would go no longer to school. By
the time he had gotten that master's he was nearly forty
years old, and he said he didn't want to go to school
anymore.

Jones: I was wondering if in leaving Tuskegee he was
rejecting Booker T. Washington's philosophy.

Alexander: I think he was. My father had no great
admiration and respect for either Booker T. Washington or George Washington Carver, or any of the other
people at Tuskegee. He felt they were flunkies and
toadies to the white man, you see; they were the great
compromisers. He liked *Souls of Black Folk*. Du Bois
was in Atlanta at the time my father was at Tuskegee;
and by the time Daddy went, in 1910, to Atlanta, Du
Bois was just leaving Atlanta. He was going then to
New York, to the NAACP and the *Crisis Magazine*.
But my father greatly admired Du Bois and everything
he stood for. He did not admire Booker T. Washington
or Carver at all. My mother did; and the strange thing
was that my father had had enough training to be able
to use his hands. He was a good tailor, and I don't
know whether he learned something about it at Tuskegee or not, but I think he already knew it, because he
practiced that trade even after he was married. My

father was a good tailor, a bookkeeper, as he said, and he knew shorthand and typing. He taught my mother some shorthand, and she was a good typist, too. But Daddy was a man interested very much in higher education, in book learning. My father was a scholar of the classical order. He even knew Latin, Greek, and Hebrew. And he was interested in languages. He spoke Spanish, and he read and spoke French; and he knew Hindustani. He could even converse with the Jewish merchants in Yiddish. That was the kind of education he admired.

Jones: Did he instill this in his family?

Alexander: Yes. As I look back upon it with my own children and my siblings, we were a family who were expected to pursue goals in higher education, always. My sisters and brother went to graduate school. The sister in New York has completed most of the work for the doctorate in music; the sister in New Orleans took two master's degrees, one from the University of Chicago in child psychology and another at Loyola at New Orleans in the teaching of science and math to little children. My brother pursued the master's in mathematics. My mother went to graduate school; so you see, we tended to look up to a professional graduate education. I have four children. All of them have had a college education. One is a lawyer, so he went to law school, beyond college years. The others still aspire to go to school. It just follows a kind of pattern in the family.

Jones: Yes. Was it your father's idea that book learning was the fastest way to racial equality?

Alexander: I don't think that was ever in his mind. I really think now, as I look back, that my father believed in learning for learning's sake, for the sake of knowledge.

Jones: Yes.

Alexander: That was the much bigger idea. My grandmother and her family aspired to middle-class citizenship and considered education a means toward it. That was the American Negro attitude. But my father was not an American Negro. He had come from out of the islands, and knowledge for the sake of knowledge was something they knew in those islands. There's a difference.

Jones: Did your father—did you ever see that he was chafing under the atmosphere that was in the South at the time that you were growing up?

Alexander: Well, I think so, yes. Once in Birmingham he was chased by a policeman who saw him with books and a fountain pen; my father had been teaching night school. He couldn't conceive of a black man as a professional man. I wrote a poem once about my father, and I said that he was always puzzled, bewildered, disturbed about race prejudice in the South. He was never prepared for it. But I don't think black people as a whole, no matter how many years we have lived here, are ever prepared for sudden racial frontal attacks. Nobody ever gets complacent about it. It's always a feeling of what could be more stupid than this, and why did people take this attitude, and when will they cease to think this way? You see, I think that's true with the average black person. The feeling of slavery and previous condition of servitude, I think it's more in the white mind than in the black mind. I don't think black people—now that we say we are a hundred and fifteen, nearly a hundred and twenty years away from slavery—I don't think the average [black person], and certainly not the black child or the young black person, slavery never enters his mind as a reason or cause for this. In writing about Richard Wright, I came upon some interesting deductions and conclusions of this man who was badly scarred by racism.

Jones: That's very interesting. You deal with this problem in your new book on Wright? [*The Daemonic Genius of Richard Wright*, to be published by Howard University Press.]

Alexander: Certain conclusions that he made, in which he seemed to feel that the only explanation for the kind of suffering and racism and racial pain the black man suffers in America, not just in the South, is an existentialist one. He says that we suffer for no reason at all, that the idea of black people suffering simply because they are black is not a reason for human suffering. It's absurd.

Jones: It is.

Alexander: An absurdity is explained best by the existentialist, you see, and he thinks that there is no justifiable reason for racial suffering in America. I think earlier he might have felt as the Marxists felt, that it was an economic determinism, that it was because of the use of slavery—to buttress rising capitalism and industrialism—that this is the reason for slavery; and that the slave-holding people, the slavers, slave masters, had to develop some kind of rationale to justify their keeping other human beings in bondage. I talk about it a great deal in *Jubilee.* I think it's a theme, a thesis, that runs through much of Afro-American literature. Do you have another question now? Are you ready to go on to something else?

Jones: I really did want to ask you some more questions about slavery and the way you use it in *Jubilee*, the way you came to conceive of it as a young writer. You know, taking graduate school history courses—I'm not so sure that that's the real correct and best image of slavery that one can get, just discussing it from a scholarly standpoint.

Alexander: Well, fiction, I think I say in a little book that I wrote called "How I Wrote *Jubilee*," I say that more people will read a story than will read the actual history books.

Jones: That's true.

Alexander: And, therefore, the novelist as a social historian, has a job to do that the historian cannot do.

Jones: Yes, ma'am, I agree.

Alexander: *Jubilee* took a long time in the writing, because I guess I had to live a lot of things before I could do the authentic writing. I didn't know how to write a novel, and I had to learn. But then I had to become saturated in the period, and I had to do a lot of research. I spent ten years in actual research, thirty years from the time I started writing that book at Northwestern until the conclusion in Iowa. Meanwhile, it had grown out of my childhood.

Jones: Yes, ma'am.

Alexander: My grandmother told the story to me when I was just a little girl sitting around at night before bedtime, or at bedtime. When I was nineteen and a senior at Northwestern, I thought I was mature enough and ready to write the novel. I had already tried to write a novel when I was about twelve, and it didn't do very well. I started this one and it didn't do very well; but I wrote about three hundred pages and then realized that I didn't know how to do it. It didn't sound right and I put it down. I had an ideal for *Jubilee*. I don't know why even—I guess it's amazing that I actually finally got through it, because I wanted it to be perfect; and I think that is a great mistake many writers make, that they want their books to be perfect—their first book or their next book or whatever; and they do as much as possible to be perfectionists. That's all very good, provided you eventually let go of the thing.

Jones: Get it down. . . .

Alexander: And leave it alone! I think Ralph Ellison's *Invisible Man* did that to him.

Jones: Yes, ma'am.

Alexander: And I really believe that is the reason that Ralph hasn't been able to finish another book, that perfectionist business.

Jones: That's right.

Alexander: I don't think Wright was as much of a
perfectionist . . . he might have been a perfectionist
because he was highly critical; but he wasn't too intro-
spective; otherwise he would not have written over and
over again the same plot.

Jones: That's right. But it was something that you
always had to grapple with as a writer, and the poem
"For My People" came from other places in your mind
than did the story of *Jubilee?*

Alexander: I don't know. You see, that's an interesting comment on the creative process. I started writing
poetry when I was about twelve or thirteen, but I had
already tried to compose prose when I was ten. I never
thought it was going to be as hard to write prose as it
was to write poetry, but as I grew older I realized that
it might sometimes be harder. Most young people, and
I think I was no exception, have the notion that poetry
is rhymed and metered writing, whereas prose is not.
And that is not really a good definition of either poetry
or prose. Good prose has as much rhythm as good
poetry, and it has its own imagery, and it has all the
same things, but the structure is different. The use of
metaphor and simile for the poet is much more necessary and involves poetic patterns that come from the
same thinking creatively as the prose patterns. It isn't
in one corner of the mind and then another corner; it's
all from the same creative thinking. And creative
thinking, all of it, begins the same way. And the artist,
whether he is visual or graphic or plastic, whether he's
a writer, a musician, an architect, or a sculptor, or
painter, regardless, he simply learns to conceive things
in terms of the unit of his work. If he's an architect, he
sees space and design; he's confronted with a certain
creative use of space. The musician has a motif, and he
hears the certain musical sounds and patterns together.
The painter sees color, line, and movement in building
a composition. And the writer has nothing but words,

you see, but he gets an idea: he has a concept first and then a thought and then an idea, and then figurations and configurations, and he's off to the races.

Jones: Yes, ma'am. It seems to me, though, that with *Jubilee* you had the great pressure of not only making sure that your work had historical integrity, getting down the slavery and events of the Civil War and Reconstruction accurately, but you also had the pressure of making it worthy to your family.

Alexander: Well, I think I'm faced with more problems with the sequel than I was with that; because people now have a certain conception and a way that they want things done, and maybe things won't always fall into those patterns. How a family feels could be very, very opposite to what you're going to do. Then they would feel that you had been unfair and unfaithful to your family heritage and maybe something there was detrimental. I don't know. I've got it in my mind and I hope I'm going to live to get it down, but it better be soon!

Jones: Right! But your poem "For My People" came out in 1942.

Alexander: No, I wrote that poem in 1937; and the book—as a thesis, I composed a thesis for my master's degree in English at Iowa in 1940, I did that book; and I won the Yale award in 1942, and that's when the book was published. [*For My People,* Yale University Press.] But the poem was five years old when the book was published. And I had written that poem sometime around my twenty-second birthday. It was written in fifteen minutes on a typewriter, with the exception of the last stanza of strophe, and then I took that to the project [WPA] and showed it to Nelson Algren, who told me that I ought to say what I wanted for my people, and then I'd have a poem; and of course I knew what I wanted to say there—another world, another whole earth to come into being. And I never changed

in the ideas of that last stanza. I wrote a number of
poems at the time in the same vein, with the same kind
of long line. My most recent book of poetry has one or
two poems in it like that, but for the most part, the
verse, my pattern of free verse, has changed greatly
since I wrote "For My People."

Jones: At the time that you sat down at the typewriter
to write "For My People" and you were twenty-two
years old, were you angry, did you feel like. . .

Alexander: No, I don't think it was anger that that
poem came out of . . . I don't think I write out of
anger. I say that is the way that Richard Wright writes;
and there's a lot of protest. I don't think my writing
has grown out of anger or hostility. I think it's grown a
great deal out of a kind of brooding, intuitive, internal
questioning and seeking answers. I don't think that
ever I was writing out of anger. I don't think so. When
I look at Wright's work and see what you produce out
of anger, I know that we were thinking differently. He
writes violently.

Jones: Yes, he does.

Alexander: And I never have done that. Both of us
have sometimes expressed revolutionary ideas, but mine
didn't come out of anger. They came out of deep con-
sideration and contemplation of problems. I think it's
been more intuitive than demonic.

Jones: Right. When you say "let a new race of men
rise and take control," it's revolutionary . . . especially
for 1937, and for a Southerner.

Alexander: The thirties . . . well, black people, black
literature, Afro-American literature was very revolutionary. It was protest literature, and Wright was the
leader of that. I knew Wright, and I think he influenced my thinking in that respect. Langston had
come through the twenties writing a very different kind
of stuff, and then in the thirties and forties he was
writing more in terms of the mood of black literature.

In the thirties it was protest. In the forties we were
getting into the war years, and the cold war years in the
fifties. And of course the forties, the fifties don't sound
like the thirties and the twenties any more than the
sixties and the seventies sound like the eighties. They're
very different. Each decade is different.

Jones: That's right. What about Richard Wright? Tell
me about meeting him. We just got through reading
Black Boy for a graduate history course that I took.

Alexander: Did you like the book?

Jones: I did, personally. It affected me personally and
made my heart bleed. It was interesting to see the
reaction that young whites have to it today, because
most of the class is made up of young whites.

Alexander: Some of them did not like it.

Jones: Some of them felt that he lacked objectivity and
that all of the white people that he encountered growing up in Mississippi in the twenties and thirties could
not have been that purely evil.

Alexander: They weren't the twenties and thirties. He
left here in '25. He was a very angry man. I don't know
why people would expect a biography to be objective.

Jones: He's not pretending to be objective.

Alexander: Not there. But I talk about *Black Boy* in
the book. And two black writers, two Afro-Americans,
have done an excellent job of criticizing the book. The
book is a social document. Today it's more than a literary work of art and a legend, it's a social document.
Black Boy is Richard Wright's youth, and he is an
angry young man. He's ambivalent and angry and
alienated and aberrated—all of those things. I think
you can see most of that in *Black Boy*.

Jones: Certainly. A great deal of the book is about
stereotypes. Most of the people that he runs into represent a stereotype of the Southerner, white or black.

Alexander: I think that's the very first thing I talk
about when—I have an essay in there that I took over

from something I did for the Mississippi Arts Festival,
and they printed it, and I'm using it in the book because I think it's a very good introduction to a side of
black, Southern literature that we haven't thought
about. That's the black side of it. We've studied the
white. Wright is very Southern, he's very Southern;
and he belongs to a definite tradition in Southern literature, which is called Southern gothic, gothicism. A
man like Faulkner belongs in it; even Miss Welty belongs in it.

Jones: Erskine Caldwell?

Alexander: Yes. They're all very much Southern
gothic. And Wright is more than that. Wright belongs
in four great traditions. He's Southern gothic; he's
American naturalist of the Middlewestern brand, natu-
ralistic writer; he's an Afro-American who's interested
in humanism, and the humanism runs through two
hundred years of Afro-American literature; and then
he's a realist. Wright is a great intellect. His intellect
was so great that his own world view incorporates five
great ideas of the twentieth century. And I don't think
even Faulkner could top that. Wright is Marxist—
everybody knows that, but Wright is Freudian; Wright
is existentialist; Wright is a pan-Africanist; and Wright
understood a great deal about industrialization, but he
didn't understand too much of the technological nature
of society, but he was trying to. So you see, those five
ideas are in his works. And that's a great intellectual
synthesis.

Jones: What about the danger—I wanted to ask you
about this later but now's fine—what about the danger
of combining? As you say, he's combined so many
ideas, the biggest ideas. Most novelists say that the
most dangerous thing and the most threatening and
harmful thing to the novel itself is didacticism and
preaching and that type of thing. Do you. . .

Alexander: Wright is not always didactic. He is

sometimes, the didacticism is there sometimes; but I think what I thought about when I was writing *Jubilee* was how much burden of history can fiction bear? You see, a lot of people think of Wright's protest novels as being thinly veiled sociology and that a novel is not that. All I ever heard people say is that a novel is not sociology, and a novel is not psychology, and a novel is not philosophy, and a novel is not history, and a novel is not all these things. But a novel is all of those; a novel has all that in it.

Jones: Did Wright influence you as a writer?

Alexander: Yes, I think he influenced me. I think I have to say he did. He didn't, as Fabre [Michel Fabre, *The Unfinished Quest of Richard Wright*] very tritely and very glibly says, "introduce me to literature." It's obvious if I had graduated from Northwestern when I met Wright, and I was a major in English literature, that he didn't introduce me to literature.

Jones: Right.

Alexander: But he did influence me because I learned not to accept dialectical materialism. I'm not a materialist—I consider myself still grounded in Christianity and the idealistic philosophy of my father and my forefathers; but I did get a different social perspective. I did begin to think more seriously about racial affairs in America, and I did get a pole of meaning around which I could integrate ideas from Wright. He and I read many of the same books. I think three black writers outside of my own family influenced me, and Wright was one of them. Langston Hughes was one and W. E. B. Du Bois was another. Those three men, I think their ideas took hold of me. I saw Langston when I was sixteen, I saw Du Bois when I was seventeen, and I saw Wright when I was twenty.

Jones: They all came to Northwestern?

Alexander: No, no. Langston came to the South and told my parents to get me out of the South so that I would develop. He came to New Orleans where they were teaching, and I guess I was instrumental in their bringing him because I wanted to see what a "real, live poet" looked like. I'd never seen one. I saw James Weldon Johnson in New Orleans, heard him read his poetry. I heard Marian Anderson and Roland Hayes. I don't think I heard Paul Robeson in the South, I think I heard him first in the North. But these were just magnificent voices. Langston—I knew him for thirty-five years, and I think I was influenced by Langston. I don't write like him, no. But we spent a lot of time together, and I have a number of books that he autographed to me. I was looking at one today that says "This is with the hope that you will continue to grow in the wonder of poetry," something like that. I believe it's right there. "For Margaret, your health, salud. Spanish Revolution."

Jones: And it goes on, "March 30, 1938, Chicago, Langston."

Alexander: And "For Margaret, with high hopes for your continued growth in the wonderland of poetry. Sincerely, Langston." That was at Atlanta University.

Jones: 1947.

Alexander: Yes. I have another little one here. It was a Christmas greeting to me and my husband, and I thought I had another one here. I had at one time sixteen books by Langston. Most of them had been autographed for me. I didn't know Du Bois nearly as intimately, or closely, as I did Langston and Wright. I saw Du Bois at Northwestern. He came there to speak. I saw Harriet Monroe at Northwestern . . . I don't have nearly as many of Du Bois's books. I'm getting ready to do a speech for the behavioral scientists' convention here, and I'm going to talk about the seminal mind of Du Bois. He's father of sociology or behavioral science; and in my estimation there are five men who are the giants of the century. Wright, of course, is taken with all of them, and I realized as I wrote a book of poetry about three years ago when I came into retirement that Marx and Freud, Kierkegaard, Einstein, and Du Bois are the five great thinkers of the century. Du Bois— everything that deals with the race, the sociology of the Negro, the history of the Negro in this country, the problems of world Negroes, the black world problems, pan-Africanism, and freedom and unity in the black world, all of that is out of Du Bois, those very great ideas there. Then Marx, of course, is the man the revolutions have all been patterned after. Socialism, there's no question, is the politics of the twentieth century. All revolutions have been based on it. Whether we like it or not, that's the way it is. Freud is the person who dug the groundwork for the understanding of self and psychology, and we've gone a long way from him; and I'm not a Freudian. I don't hold to him: Freud is no good for women. I like what Karen Horney says about psychoanalysis and about the neurotic personality of our time, and about personality, period. Wright and I believed very differently about personality; he believed the Freudian ideas of creativity, of art, of sex, of everything, you see, whereas I think the best of Freud is his groundwork for psychoanalysis. That's it. I don't think he understood women at all.

Jones: You were going on to define how you differ from Wright.

Alexander: Well, I differ from Wright in psychology and philosophy. I'm not a materialist. All of his life, from Marxism on, Wright was interested in the materialist stance in philosophy. But I am not a materialist at all. I think that in economics Marx is sound, but I think he is spiritually bankrupt and he can't work a philosophy in the same way that I would not branch off with Hegel as Marx does. You see, Hegel goes two ways. I would rather go along with Emmanuel Kant than Hegel. That's a way that we differ, very, very much so. Our perspectives differ, too, in that I'm a woman and he was a man, though I think he was as ambivalent sexually as he was racially, socially, or politically. And that's saying a lot, but I think I've come up with that. I think that what happens to black and white men in the South is a very, very serious psychological problem. I think that there is an aberration that comes out of the aberrational South, in that there's a mirror image of racism in the South, that what white men see in black men, black men see in white men. Have you ever thought about that?

Jones: I've never thought about it, no.

Alexander: What happens is that there is a kind of sexual warfare in the South between black and white men over their women. Everybody understands that.

Jones: Yes, ma'am. Certainly. The cult of Southern womanhood and all of that.

Alexander: Yes, all of that. And the black man in Mississippi particularly, is eaten up with the same kind of racism that the white man is. He, and Wright was— they suffer from all the problems of the racist sexual warfare, and race and sex become corollaries in the South. And I don't know why it hasn't—it dawns on me, I haven't read it anywhere, I haven't seen it, but the more I read Wright the more I realize what had happened to him; and of course, I have Wendell Berry, *The Hidden Wound*, in which he says if the white man inflicted racism on the black man he got it in himself at the same time, because there's a mirror image; and he couldn't hate this man without bringing some of that . . .

Jones: Hatred into his own life. Is that what you mean?

Alexander: That's part of it. But that mirror image of racism—the worst thing for the white man in the Deep South, the Southern white man, the worst thing in the world was a black man with a white woman.

140

Jones: Sure.

Alexander: For the black man, the worst thing in the world was a black woman with a white man. Same thing. See, same thing, isn't it?

Jones: But the black man, in his entire experience in America, had been used to seeing his black woman with a white man all through slavery.

Alexander: Yes, but wait a minute, wait a minute. It's not that he got accustomed to it; he never did. He was mad about it all the time. It was a part of his anger, part of black rage, you see, and he was living with the white man. That's part of his black rage. And for the white man, he said any day he catches that black man with a white woman, he will lynch him. So he's got the rage, too, hasn't he?

Jones: Yes, ma'am, I understand what you mean.

Alexander: It's there, and it's been there a long time. The problem won't be suppressed. You have a philosophy of race that says there's superiority and inferiority; an oppressed people who develop a sense of inferiority, because they are told that so long. This is denigrating and denying humanity; and it affects the psyche of the black male. It hurts him worse than it does the black woman, though she's affected too. The white woman is affected in a different way from the black woman; therefore, you have in the women's liberation movement two strains. That Southern white woman's quest for liberation is very different from that Northern or that Southern black woman's quest for liberation. They're not moving down the same path. They don't have the same goals; they're not of the same mind.

Jones: Yes. Perhaps that accounts for the way the women's movement is fragmented and hasn't been successful in a lot of areas.

Alexander: As long as it went along in a universal way with the civil rights movement and the movement for black liberation and the movement of all people, the gay business and all of that, it's all right, as long as everybody wants to be free. But when you come to certain segmented sections of it . . . .

Jones: And you said that the kind of bitterness and outrage that grew within Wright about the problems of sex and the South and the other problems . . . .

Alexander: They aberrate him, they make him aberrant. For example, take that child, that black boy in Atlanta. The white papers scream out right away that this is a homosexual, but I don't think anybody understands that that's deep in the Southern culture, to say that any time you have a very brilliant, smart, intellectual black, that he's gay.

Jones: Yes, gay.

Alexander: And as Leroi Jones said, "White man called us faggots until the end of our lives." I remember the very first time that anybody approached me with the idea of—a white fellow in Iowa who was married to a black woman, at least they were living together whether they were married or not, said to me, "Why is it that all black intellectual men are so emasculated?" I said, "Are they?" My father was intellectual, a scholar, and I didn't think of him as emasculated at all. Do you see? It's deep in the culture.

Jones: Yes, ma'am. I did want to ask you—I know that all during the early 1960s you were in the process of writing *Jubilee* in the final form, but what about what took place here in Mississippi in the sixties, the early sixties, with the violence and the civil rights workers coming in, how did that affect you? I know you were at Jackson State.

Alexander: Well, I wasn't here. I found myself in an untenable position in the early sixties. My students were in revolt, and the administration was holding the line for segregation on orders of the powers that be—shall we say, the establishment. And like most of the teachers, I was called in and asked whether I was on the side of the students or on the side of the administration. And I said I couldn't take either side. If I sided with my students against the administration, I wouldn't have a job; and if I sided with the administration against the students, I wouldn't have anybody to teach, and I wouldn't be able to do that either. So I went to school. I was ill in the summer of '60, in the hospital, so in '61 I went out to Iowa, and I came back in the state through a hellish year, '61 and '62, but the fall of '62 I was in Iowa and I stayed there three years. And I came back, and it was still going on. But I was gone the most violent year of all. 1963 was the most violent year.

Jones: The death of Medgar Evers.

Alexander: Yes. Kennedy was killed, the march on Washington, the children bombed in the church in Birmingham—it was a violent year, it was a horrible year. Then in '65 they killed Malcolm X; and in '68 both King and Bobby Kennedy. All of the sixties were violent. But '63 was the worst year of all.

Jones: Do you remember it as a time of great excitement? Were you excited about what black people were finally doing?

Alexander: I think it was a time of sheer terror and, well, there were some things you liked, and some things you were afraid of. There were times you were just plain fearful of what was going to happen. I was here in the summer of '64. We hadn't remodeled the house; we didn't have this part of the house. And I would sit out under the tree and read for my comprehensives. That was the summer that the civil rights workers were murdered.

Jones: Goodman and Schwerner [and Chaney].

Alexander: Goodman and Schwerner and Chaney were killed over there out from Philadelphia, and everybody said they were going to find out that . . . and, of course, Dulles [Allen Dulles] came down here and said it. It was clandestine. . . .

Jones: Civil rights activities.

Alexander: Civil rights activities. Subversive activities of the Klan; the Ku Klux Klan did that.

Jones: Yes. Right.

Alexander: That wasn't the civil rights workers. I lived in a neighborhood here where a lot of civil rights workers from out of the state came and stayed in here. One night I kept the daughter of a Tufts professor and doctor, and I was afraid. I told her, "Oh, you can't get out on the road now and go." You know, coming out of a black community and going back there. I said, "You'll have to wait till morning." And I kept her overnight. But nobody knew when people were in here.

Jones: Yes, that's right.

Alexander: I don't think I had nearly the problems in the sixties that I had in the seventies. My problems were very great in the seventies. The whole decade of the seventies was personally traumatic for me. My son was caught up in the RNA [Republic of New Africa] stuff, and two students were killed at Jackson State.

Jones: May of '70.

Alexander: That's right. My son was in Vietnam and came home in '70; another son in law school came very nearly being killed. His car was totally wrecked; people had deliberately run into him. Oh, I just went . . . I had it in the seventies—ending up with *Roots* [the controversy over *Roots* and its alleged plagiarism from *Jubilee*].

Jones: Yes, ma'am.

Alexander: I was supposed to go abroad on a Fulbright, and I couldn't leave home. I don't think the decade of the sixties was nearly as traumatic for me as the decade of the seventies.

Jones: I read a book, conversations between you and Nikki Giovanni.

Alexander: Did you like that?

Jones: I enjoyed that very much, but I was—I know what you mean when you say that it was a traumatic time for you because of the conflicts between a young

black writer who was the product of the sixties and all
the turmoil at that time.

Alexander: I heard from Nikki last week, and I was
surprised because I hadn't heard from her in almost a
year. Everybody says she's mellowing. I don't think I'm
mellowing at all!

Jones: The conflict between your traditional Christian
values, the Christian tradition that you grew out of,
and the tradition of the sixties that produced Nikki
Giovanni and her generation of poets—it was a fascinating kind of confrontation between the two of you.
Black culture, the whole face of black existence, was
changing at that time. Wasn't it?

Alexander: Well, in a way yes and in a way not.
What was it, the saying—the more things change the
more they seem to remain the same. Change, yes, but
not enough change. Perhaps the eighties will be even
more difficult than any of those decades, because we are
in such an economic pit. I don't see us getting out of
that economic pit; and the political reins are pulling
tighter into neo-conservatism. What Reagan is setting
up can last an awful long time. Of course, black people
are not going to be able to change it by themselves. It
will take thinking white people to change it, too.

Jones: Yes, ma'am. What does it mean for the black
artist?

Alexander: Well, for me, I don't know what's going
to happen when the book on Richard Wright comes
out. I don't know. I wondered what would happen
when *Jubilee* came out. I didn't expect it to be as well
received as it was. It sold into the millions of copies.
People used to say to me, "If you have trouble in Mississippi, you'd just leave, wouldn't you?" I'd say,
"Yes." But then I had trouble and I didn't leave, because I contended there was no place to go where it was
any better. Might be terribly bad here, but show me
where it's better!

Jones: Are you glad you made that choice?

Alexander: Oh, I think Mississippi has been good for me all along. I'm glad I made the decision to come to Mississippi, and I'm glad I've stayed here. It's given me the pace I needed. I couldn't take the pace of New York. I don't like New England. I don't like cold weather for one thing. But that's not all of it. Climate of opinion. You hardly have anybody to talk to. There's nobody to raise an intellectual issue with you. That's the truth.

Jones: Is it?

Alexander: That's the truth. The few black and white people I know who are intellectually of some size or some stature are too busy to be bothered most of the time. Of course, the condition of the country is the same everywhere. You pick up the newspaper, and you're just about as well off—I don't see the New York papers and I don't see the Washington papers, almost never anymore. It used to be that if you didn't see those papers, you didn't know what was going on. "There ain't nothing going on, see?" And I'd just as soon be in Jackson, Mississippi, as Podunk, New York. But it is a sad state of affairs. And education in the country is a disaster area. We're certainly not going forward. If we're not going backward, we must be standing still.

Jones: We could talk for a lot longer, if we had time.

Alexander: I have been known to go on for a twenty-four-hour stretch, but I'm tired now.

Jones: I know you're tired. I'm sorry to have kept you so long. And thank you.

Photograph by Mark Morrow

James Whitehead

November 17, 1980

I'd known Jim Whitehead for a good many years before we met at my parents' home for this interview. He and my father were classmates at Jackson's old Central High, and his wife Gen is a distant cousin of my mother's. The families saw a good bit of each other as I was growing up. What I remembered about him from those years before I knew he was a working writer was the power of his physical presence, the way his six-foot-six frame and his booming voice made him seem larger than life. When we met again in 1980 after I'd come to know him through his work, I found that none of those qualities I remembered had diminished in him. He had more gray hairs, but still there was the energy, the appetite for life and learning which he brought to Sonny Joiner and the characters in his poems. This interview was done in my parents' living room in Jackson on a rainy Monday afternoon in mid-November. It lasted almost four hours. Understandably, some cuts were made for publication. We could have gone on, but he'd told me beforehand that he wanted to interview in the afternoon, visit with my folks awhile in the early evening, and then take Tom Royals and me to dinner that night.

Jones: As I told you, Jim, I'd like to just start off and get some of your early biographical information, something about when and where you were born, your parents, education, and that type of thing.

Whitehead: I was born March 15, 1936, in St. Louis, Missouri. My father was born in Bonne Terre, Missouri. My mother was born in Springfield, Missouri. One is on the western end of the Ozarks—Springfield, of course; and Bonne Terre is over in the eastern part of the Ozarks. Daddy graduated from the ag school at the University of Missouri, then went to work in St. Louis. Mama has her degree in social work from Missouri. We moved to Memphis, I believe, in 1940 and then to Hattiesburg in 1941. We were there on December 7, 1941. We were fishing on the Coast, and I remember I caught a drum fish, you know?

Jones: Yes.

Whitehead: And we got back in from fishing, and the women were back at the house in a great stir because the news had come about the war. Daddy must have gone into the service within six months, but it may have been six weeks. At that point we moved to New York state, to Georgia, back to Missouri while he was in Europe. He had an extraordinary war career from Le Havre to Berlin. Then after the war I think he took a semester and did some work past his master's, and then we came back to Hattiesburg. I was in the fifth grade. And then we moved to Jackson. My grandmother, who night before last had her hundredth birthday party . . .

Jones: I need to interview her.

Whitehead: Now that is the God's truth!

Jones: Was her father in the Civil War? Is that in the poem "Domains"?

Whitehead: Her grandfather. Let's see, was it her father or grandfather? Yes, it was her grandfather, a Dr. Bourland on her mother's side, who was a Confederate surgeon during the Civil War. He was a great character, a writer, who wrote a book called *Entolai*, which I believe in Greek is "The Wisdom" or "The Story of My Life." It's a prose romance between one character who represents the life of practical activity and science and the other who represents the life of the spirit, the ideal. It's really a rather terrible and wonderful book at the same time.

Jones: Yes, in your poem "Domains" you mention him. There's also the mention in "Domains" of a Union officer in your family.

Whitehead: That's the Whitehead side of the family, the Ozark Republican side of the family. The Whiteheads were farmers down there in the lead belt in the eastern Ozarks, and apparently they were all in the Union.

Jones: It's interesting how family stories turn up in people's work.

Whitehead: You've got to watch that though, as you know, coming from the family you come from. Everybody wants to go through the book and write down, "Well, this is from that and this is from that." The problem is that too many kin read everything autobiographically, and that's not necessarily so. You write one book in which the wife of the protagonist is a saint, and everybody says that's autobiographical, which is not necessarily so. Then you write one in which she's a boozer and far from being a saint, possibly. Well, that instantly also turns out to be autobiographical, and that's not true either.

Jones: There's a new book out now by Richard King called *Southern Renaissance* which tries to explain the glut of Southern writers from 1925 to 1955.

Whitehead: Why do you say glut?

Jones: The preponderance, maybe?

Whitehead: Glut suggests a surfeit.

Jones: Yes.

Whitehead: And that sounds like a gaggle of geese. A preponderance of writers. A pod of whales.

Jones: A whole lot of writers.

Whitehead: A whole bunch, yes.

Jones: He's trying to explain the whole mess of Southern fiction produced between those years.

Whitehead: Are they still doing books on that?

Jones: Yes.

Whitehead: I mean has somebody actually published another book of that?

Jones: Yes. His explanation was that these writers were attempting to come to grips with the great Southern family romance, and somehow put history to rest.

Whitehead: I didn't really begin to understand my family until I was well grown, and really have learned more about it in the last ten years than at any other time. I'm not talking about what is unfortunately called the "nuclear family" of my Mom and Daddy and brother, but the larger family from southern Missouri and elsewhere. I didn't understand that family when I was growing up, and I've never written about it, to speak of. I don't know if I ever will. I might.

Jones: While we're on the subject though, do you have your own explanation for the '25 to '55 phenomenon in American letters?

Whitehead: I went through this at the Southern Literary Festival in Columbus this spring, this question of '25 to '55. Andrew Lytle and Dan Young were trying to do that thing where they cut it off at '55. It sounds self-serving on my part to say that it did not stop in '55, but if that's self-serving, let it be that; that's fine with me. Eudora had done a great deal of her work before '55, but an awful lot of her important work is after '55. O'Conner is after '55. Foote is after '55. Percy is after '55. Jim Dickey, John Yount, on and on, you name it. I'll even say Shirley Ann Grau, who is not the most popular writer around but one I think has written some excellent books.

Jones: I don't know her.

Whitehead: She's a New Orleans writer. *House on Col-*

iseum Street is one book and *The Condor Passes* is another
one. She writes a book every two years, and I've read
several of them. She's good. That business of '25 to '55
is part of the literary industry. Barry Hannah, George
Garrett, Fred Chappell, many, many more.
Jones: Right.
Whitehead: Miller Williams. Alice Walker: a marvelous writer, black woman writer from Georgia. That
cutoff at '55—what I did at the literary festival, when
they were putting this over to a bunch of young people,
was read from *Southern Writers: A Biographical Dictionary*
that L.S.U. published. Have you seen it?
Jones: Sure.
Whitehead: And there was supposed to be a debate,
and in a sense it was. Mr. Lytle, who is to be revered as
an important critic, and he has written several marvelous books, did the usual shuck-and-jive about the death
of it all in '55. Whatever happened in '55 I don't
know. So I just simply read the names of writers. I had
five minutes, five minutes, and I read names for five
minutes from James Agee to Al Young. Do you know
Al's work?
Jones: No.
Whitehead: From Pass Christian, Mississippi, black,
lives in San Francisco, and writes beautifully about
growing up in Mississippi. So that whole business
about the academic critic wanting to shut the gate on
the generation prior to me, on my generation, and on
the young people I'm working with and encouraging, is
something I think ought to be rejected out of hand,
dismissed, and considered. Lord, what do you say about
it? What's the point in that? My point is not to make a
case for more things "Southern." I'm not interested in
that. What I'm interested in is art, in literature. We
have an Acadian literature that has hardly been
translated yet. In the Chicano part of the South—Texas
is a Southern state—you have a tremendous literature

that has just been born in the last twenty-five years. It is a brand new thing! Where do these people get off saying that these people are not making discoveries? Of course, one of the things they say is that the racial issue in the South has been laid to rest. The racial issue is not solved. The problems endure, and they will endure for a long time. It's a condition. Whew!

Jones: Yes.

Whitehead: All right. Now, if you want to talk about that book anymore, it's all right with me. I haven't read the book and won't! I mean, I've read that book! Twenty-four times!

Jones: And it's a favorite subject of literary buffs, so I'd just as soon leave it alone. I do want to talk later about the role of the academic world in the creative process.

Whitehead: I'm against pedantry. Most scholars, critics, and writers are against it. Possibly a majority. I was not saying anything bad about going to school and getting an education. That's the last thing I would do. I was talking about a particular brand of academic critic who has a vested interest in a group of writers who lived and produced their work between certain dates. It has to do, for example, with the apotheosis of Mr. Faulkner. The entire Faulkner industry is part of it, which is fine. Faulkner is a very great writer, but he's been mistreated by critics, been misunderstood by his critics, and he has been used as a way to stifle anyone who might have grown up in his shadow. That's something he would've never done, never!

Jones: Do you think his contribution to American letters has been exaggerated?

Whitehead: John Yount says he's the greatest American novelist. I don't like to make lists of who is the greatest and who is second, third or fourth. It's not a horse race. I don't know whether Eliot or Auden said that. He's a very great novelist. Melville is a rather good novelist, right?

Jones: Yes.

Whitehead: And someone he is frequently compared with, I suppose.

Jones: Did he influence your writing?

Whitehead: Well, as I told the people here at the program I did a month ago at the Mississippi Council of Teachers of English—fine group of people—that Faulkner is like the humidity in Mississippi. You don't avoid Mr. Faulkner, you grow up with him. And sure, I read him and loved it and made a pilgrimage when I was a junior, I think, in college. I'd just written and published my first short story. I went to Oxford and found him sitting on his front steps, talked to him with a couple of other fellows for a couple of hours. He talked mainly to them. He even invited us to cut hay with him. I would have cut hay for days with Mr. Faulkner, of course, but a storm came up and that was that and we went on. I love him, love his work. As far as my own writing, no, I don't think it's been radically influenced by him more than anyone else. You know, he'd read King James English and was subject to Southern rhetoric, had read Dickens, and Dostoyevsky and Tolstoy in translation, and detective novels and all the rest. Sure, there's a kind of influence. I told the people out there that if I were to think about people who really stuck in my head over the years, more recently, since Mr. Faulkner, I'd have to say someone like Joyce Cary or Henry Miller. I tend to read Cary more for sensuality and Miller more for the descriptions of nature; which I think may be a bit backward from the way some people read them.

Jones: Henry Miller wrote *Tropic of Cancer* and *Tropic of Capricorn*.

Whitehead: The dirty writer.

Jones: Right, whose books were banned in places. Now, you mentioned to me once that Henry James had an influence on you greater than Faulkner.

Whitehead: I never mentioned Henry James to you.

Jones: Yes, last summer in the kitchen. I think I'm telling the truth.

Whitehead: I don't think I ever mentioned Henry James to you. I think I said Henry Miller, yes.

Jones: Okay.

Whitehead: I don't think I've mentioned the name Henry James very often in my lifetime. No, I do remember that conversation we had, and I said Miller. Well, I know I said Henry Miller, and then I said Joyce Cary, and you might have transposed it to James Joyce. I don't know.

Jones: Well, since then I've been wrestling in my mind with what kind of influence Henry James could have had on Jim Whitehead.

Whitehead: I'm sure. And, truly, I should pay more attention to Henry James.

Jones: James was an expatriate who was always criticized for writing about a section of the country, the East coast, that didn't really represent the American spirit and that he didn't really love.

Whitehead: You don't have to love a region—well, love? Sure, you have to have some intense relationship. Do you mean New England and New York?

Jones: Yes.

Whitehead: Well, he grew up in it.

Jones: And by the mid 1870s left it for good except for occasional visits.

Whitehead: Well, Warren has been away from Guthrie, Kentucky—it is Guthrie, isn't it?

Jones: Yes.

Whitehead: He's been away from Guthrie forever and he's still writing poems about his mother and father and the mill there. He's doing his best recollections of Guthrie in his seventies.

Jones: Fifty years away from it.

Whitehead: Yes, sure. Oh, at least. He left when he was sixteen to go to Vanderbilt. I believe he was a sixteen-year-old freshman.

156

Jones: Let me return to the chronology of your life for a minute. You came to Jackson and began what grade?

Whitehead: Seventh. Wrong. Sixth grade. Liberty Grove Elementary School, except it wasn't elementary at all. It was a ten-grade school. There were a good many of them in the state at that time. What do they call that now? It's not Watkins?

Jones: Yes. And then you started at Central?

Whitehead: No, I went to Bailey Junior High in the eighth and ninth grades. And then I went to Central all the way through.

Jones: Were you a serious student at that age?

Whitehead: No, I was very scattered and uneven. I read a good deal. I was a very uneven student. I had good teachers in literature. I read a lot of history and geography. I read the Bible, of course. I've always been an uneven student. I've made relatively few C's in my life.

Jones: Either D's or A's.

Whitehead: Or F's.

Jones: Reminds me of somebody I know well. Were you a serious athlete?

Whitehead: Oh, yes.

Jones: Played football all the way through.

Whitehead: Oh, yes.

Jones: Did you have good teams?

Whitehead: Oh, yes. We never won the Big 8 in those years. I think we came in second all those years; maybe second my sophomore year and second the next year. That's correct. We lost the Big 8 championship to Brookhaven in '51. Lost to Hattiesburg in '52.

Jones: And you went to Vanderbilt on a football scholarship?

Whitehead: Yes, right.

Jones: Did you play all four years there?

Whitehead: No. I got hurt my freshman year, and was red-shirted my sophomore year. That left me three more years. I came back and attended practice for two years and played very little. I had a bad arm. I had to play with a chain to hold my arm in slot. That was back in the days—I believe for four years after World War II, they had one platoon football in the NCAA. It was '54 to '58, which was the time I was there. I could manage it fairly well on offense, but . . .

Jones: Couldn't tackle.

Whitehead: Well, I could, but there is a certain limitation if you can't get your arm extended all the way on the right side.

Jones: Was it there that you discovered literature?

Whitehead: I had written stories, a story at least, in high school for the literary magazine. It was rejected. I was very much involved in the church and signed up to be a preacher, and so I'd written a lot of devotional material when I was under the care of Presbytery—that's what it's called, preordination in the Presbyterian church. I believe I took preordination under the care of Presbytery in '54, and I think I got out in '56, my sophomore year at Vanderbilt. So I wrote sermons to preach. One of the last sermons I gave I wrote in iambic pentameter. I believe it was the last sermon I ever gave. It was in blank verse.

Jones: But you did deliver sermons to congregations?

Whitehead: Yes.

Jones: I certainly never knew that.

Whitehead: Yes.

Jones: I knew Sonny could do it. He did it right at the end of the book. [*Joiner*]

Whitehead: Yes, but you don't have to have been under the care of Presbytery to do that. Most of the best preachers in Mississippi don't preach in churches!

Jones: But he had that black inflection, that country preaching sound: God-uh, Je-sus-uh.

Whitehead: Why sure. You can almost learn enough about that to write it by listening to it on Sunday morning radio. Such preaching by both black and white people.

James Whitehead

Jones: What teachers were at Vanderbilt at that time that influenced you?

Whitehead: Donald Davidson. I did most of my master's with him. Walter Sullivan. In the philosophy department, which was my undergraduate major: Philip Hallie, Samuel Stumpf, John Compton. In the English Department: a man named Cyrus Hoy who went on to be a marvelous scholar and I believe is still head of graduate studies at the University of Rochester. He was a young professor at Vanderbilt in those days. I took Spenser and Milton from him. I may have had Renaissance Non-dramatic under him, but I don't think I took that until I was in graduate school under Davidson. Great teachers. Alexander Marchant and Herbert Weaver in history. Vanderbilt was a horrifying, hellacious, soul-wrenching experience for a couple of years. I hated it! By the time I got to be a junior, things improved. During the last three years there, I met my friends. I had found out where I was to be, to a certain extent, in the world. So the last three years were, in the main, very, very good. I met John Yount, Bill Harrison, Miller Williams, who was not a student there but was passing through town as a textbook salesman. John and Miller and Bill and Robert Sorrels, a writer who lives in South Carolina; Malcolm Glass was not really in our group but a fellow we saw every now and then; George Core, who's presently the editor of the *Sewanee Review*, a marvelous woman named Melinda Maxfield. Tom McNair was there for a while. We had a great time and a lot of pain and trouble, love and trouble. But that was good. Things had fallen out and at least I had some rough, crude sense of direction by that time. I was trying to write. And I'd met Gen, the good luck of my life.

Jones: Fallen out in terms of football?

Whitehead: Yes. I'd lost my game, which was a terrible, terrible experience. I'd left the church, which was equally bad. I had gone through a couple of young loves and lost the light of my life at one point. I lost a lesser light or two. A combination of losing my high school sweetheart, my religion, and my game was a relatively devastating experience.

Jones: All in one year?

Whitehead: Pretty well, yes, pretty well all in one year.

Jones: Sophomore year?

Whitehead: Freshman year. I've never gotten over the interest in theology, nor do I want to or have any intent to give it up.

Jones: There's food for thought. I did want to ask you, if you wouldn't mind telling me, what went into your fall from grace from the Presbyterian church.

Whitehead: Well, I'm hoping it wasn't a fall from grace. Grace is an important word to me and a terribly important experience for all of us. I don't think it was fall from grace. I think it was an inability to accept a particular theology of Protestant Christianity. I didn't believe it. I mean I simply didn't believe what it said about the way the world was and the description of the world. You know, I was interested in science and all of it: philosophy, history. So I couldn't do it. I tried to be a Catholic and I tried to be an Anglican; you name it, I tried to be it. I would do pretty well with the Catholic Church, and then I'd flunk the final because it always finally got down to the Christology and special revelation. There was really no way around special revelation; you had to believe it or you were out. I did great at everything else, but I flunked the special revelation test in every denomination, every creed.

Jones: Couldn't make it when they put you in the woods to fast until you saw your vision?

Whitehead: You didn't have to be in the woods to be aware that something strange is going on and that we're in the midst of something very strange, that we're in the midst of God.

Jones: Right. Tell me when you graduated from college.

Whitehead: I was supposed to graduate in '58, but I graduated in '59. My last semester there I was taking some undergraduate courses and some graduate courses. I got my M.A. in 1960.

Jones: With the intention at that time to write?

Whitehead: Yes. I did a creative thesis, a novel. And then I came down here, came back to Jackson to teach at Millsaps.

Jones: Your Vanderbilt novel, did it contain pieces of *Joiner*?

Whitehead: I haven't read it in so many years. It was long, that's for sure. It was about four or five hundred pages. It's probably in a drawer somewhere. I have the thesis part of it. I didn't know enough to write a novel. I didn't know enough words. I didn't understand. The protagonist's name was Jack Karsh, and whether he has anything to do with Sonny Joiner, I don't know. I doubt it. But there's got to be some sort of family relationship between those characters. Karsh was a much more melancholy, droopy youth. He was puerile in many ways. If it had anything in common with what I've done since, it was nature, the description of landscape and woods and pine forests and that sort of thing. That has stuck, because I worked in the lumber mills from the time I was either sixteen to twenty or fifteen to twenty—I think I was fifteen. I'm not sure when I first went to work for the Hood Manufacturing Company in the summers. It used to be out here off Gallatin Street.

Jones: The lumber mill?

Whitehead: Yes.

Jones: How old were you?

Whitehead: I don't know. I was either fifteen or sixteen. I was underage for driving a truck. I had my regular driver's license, but no commercial license, and

I drove bob-tail lumber trucks, and they said, "To hell with it. If you get arrested, we'll cover for you." I didn't have a commercial license until I was eighteen, but I drove for at least two years without one. I worked in the mill, on the trucks, and also cruised timber. I believe the man's name I worked with in the forest was Wyatt Boyette, dead now, I believe, and a Sewanee/-Yale graduate—Yale forestry is very good—a man here in town named Jim Petty. I believe that was his name. He was a marvelous man. Wyatt Boyette was a great guy. They were the men I worked with in the woods.

Jones: Black?

Whitehead: White. I also worked on the dry chain, stacked with the blacks and the cons really. A lot of people worked there at the lumber mill who couldn't get work anywhere else.

Jones: Yes. One of the interesting things I've heard you say is that *Joiner* was the novel you wanted to write at twenty-one, but at twenty-one you didn't know the names of things—the names of trees.

Whitehead: That's what I've just said in another way, I suppose. Right. That's a great deal of it.

Jones: Do you think a young writer has got to get bad writing out of him early?

Whitehead: I think you have to get bad writing out of you all your life.

Jones: Do you think it was important for you at that age to be writing, to be working toward something without the proper tools?

Whitehead: Sure. You have to sit down and work. Tom McNair and I, one summer when we were in college, somewhere in there, after work—when was it? Lord, I don't remember—we would write in the evenings, five, six, seven hours of a night in the room. Tom was a great disciplinarian. He was a good coach for me at that time. All of that, sure, all of that was part of the discipline.

Jones: Were you writing poetry?

Whitehead: Yes.

Jones: Has poetry always been something that's easier for you to write, something that's easier to find the voice for? Is it just as difficult?

Whitehead: Yes, it's just as difficult, but difficult in a different way. In the poem you fail rapidly, in the novel you fail at great length and over a much longer period of time.

Jones: What was the first thing you had published, a poem or short story?

Whitehead: I published in the Vanderbilt literary magazine called *The Vagabond* finally. Well, I ended up publishing a number of things in *The Vagabond*—some fiction, some poetry, more poetry. I guess away from school publications, the first fiction I did was with *Nimrod* magazine, which is still extant, at the University of Tulsa. I published my first poem, I believe, in a magazine called *Quicksilver*, which was a nice little magazine that did some pretty good stuff. It was published in Texas for years and years. I don't remember my poem, but I remember it was across the page from a very rowdy and wonderful poem by Charles Bukowski. My little poem sat there and quivered and talked about ennui and sadness, and Bukowski's was a sort of bull-riding, cowboy sort of thing, not great in structure but very high in energy. I met Bukowski later and we laughed about it. It was the first time it occurred to me—I knew you were in there with other poems in a magazine, but facing across the page this rather good poem taught me a lesson.

Jones: A raunchy poem?

Whitehead: It was sort of raunchy. It wasn't one of his throw-up-in-the-elevator poems, but it was pretty rough, Bukowski's poem.

Jones: Who did influence that quality in you, that style of writing? I've always liked how you take the way people really speak and use it in your art.

Whitehead: I don't know. It's a heightening, to a

certain extent, of the way people talk. One of the great things about the way we are is that we mix levels of rhetoric. That mixing of levels of rhetoric—you can find it in a great deal of the world's literature, can't you?

Jones: Yes.

Whitehead: A recent example of it, of course, would be somebody like Anthony Burgess. Cary, of course, could do it. The British don't do it as much as they used to. American writers have always done it: Twain, right?

Jones: Yes. And I think you and Barry Hannah use it better than most.

Whitehead: Well, a great many American writers do it. Harry Crews is good at it. You find a character, you find an action, you begin to live with people in books. However they want to be, you'd best let them be, and you'd best figure out how to fashion those voices in that odd way that characters tell you they want to be fashioned. You are not taking dictation. It's not automatic writing, by any means. Lord knows it's not automatic writing or I'd have written more books. You have to be very attentive to what the characters want to become and the way the story wants to go. Maybe the proof for original sin has to do with the fact that we know what we should do in a book and yet we do not do it very often. You have to keep overcoming this tendency to want to go somewhere other than the book does.

Jones: That's good. So you were at Millsaps from '60 to '63.

Whitehead: To '63. I got married in '59 to Guendaline Graeber from Yazoo City, whom I met in summer school at Millsaps in the summer of 1957, I believe it was. She went to the W [Mississippi University for Women], graduated in three years, and either went to Millsaps two or three summers—I think it was two summers—and got through in three years.

Jones: You were teaching at the time you were at Millsaps?

Whitehead: Later I taught at Millsaps.

Jones: Tell me about those years at Millsaps.

Whitehead: It was terrific. It was the best graduate education I've ever had. I did graduate work at Vanderbilt, I did graduate work at the University of Iowa, and I did three years' graduate work at Millsaps while teaching. At Millsaps it was fifteen hours a semester, but one semester I had to teach eighteen hours. I studied with Bob Padgett. I don't know whether I would've survived those three years without him.

Jones: Was he just starting at that time?

Whitehead: We came here at the same time. He came as an A.B.D. [All But Dissertation] and I came as an M.A. We had met once or twice on the Vanderbilt campus. We had mutual friends but had not known each other in Nashville.

Jones: Did he help you with your writing at that time?

Whitehead: He read some of the things I wrote at Millsaps and was nice about them. Mainly we prepared our lessons and talked about literature. We read our lessons together. He would be preparing his courses and he would teach me while he was studying—see, I came out of Vanderbilt with an M.A. in English, but I had a philosophy B.A. with a minor in history and a minor in English. I didn't know very much! But I studied all the time. I studied fanatically. I studied without ceasing. I finally became a student. I remember the first time I gave a lecture in sophomore survey and I had not told the class everything that I knew about the subject of the day. The students didn't know that at the time, so it all seemed pretty good because it was all there outlined, and I suppose the lecture was okay. But it was a great relief to walk out of the classroom finally in survey and realize that I might have been able to talk for another five minutes.

Jones: Have something left to say.

Whitehead: That's right.

Jones: Yes, Bob Padgett taught me at Millsaps, too, and I like him very much. My mother always says he's one of the most erudite men she's ever known.

Whitehead: He's a brilliant man. He is a wonderful literary man. I dedicated *Joiner* to him.

Jones: Right. And he read some of the early drafts?

Whitehead: Yes, he did. He said a funny thing. I am going to have to give him the draft of the novel I'm working on now. It's very thin. He was very kind to *Joiner* in its early stages, and I think a bit confused about why I had sold it or how I had sold it. It didn't seem saleable, I suspect. He said after I finished *Joiner* that he was surprised to see how it had become more complicated and richer, which I think meant that it was possibly worthy of publication by the time I'd finished it. He's a gentle and kind man. He likes the novel well enough, but he had seen it through—he'd read at least parts of two drafts of the three or four or five drafts the book went through.

Jones: And here he was, a Shakespeare scholar.

Whitehead: Oh, you know, he reads everything. He's up on everything. He's not as much a fan of contemporary poetry as he is of drama and the novel. Of course, dramatic literature is really his forte.

Jones: Well, tell me how *Domains* came about. Was it a collection of poems from your early days as a writer?

Whitehead: No. I wrote my first real poems during my third year at Millsaps. I'd published several by that time, but they were exercises, greatly influenced by other people. Influences that didn't work for me. Until my third year at Millsaps, my work did not go well. I would try to find time to write, but there wasn't much time. Weekends once in a while—Christmas vacation—an odd hour in the middle of the night. I would sit down at a desk my father had made from a door.

This is the by-God truth, I just now realized this: that's
the door in *Joiner*, that's that table in *Joiner*.
Jones: Yes, that's right. In Dallas, in the apartment
with Mary Ann.
Whitehead: And I must have known that at some
time when I was writing *Joiner*, but it came back just
then, honest. We had that door-table, and I sat in front
of the window there on Marshall Street and I wrote
poetry a whole vacation. Absolutely horrible stuff! I
wrote all day, I sat there and wrote. I don't think I've
ever been so frustrated in my life. I'd written better
than what I was doing. It was just all wretched! It was
contorted. The music was bad. The ideas were clotted.
It was a mess. I despaired. That was one of the few
times in my life when I despaired. But I wrote, I wrote
the whole time. Sometime later, in the spring, I began
to read Browning. I was teaching Browning in survey
and I said, "I've got to get rid of all my influences. I've
got to quit reading all of them: Dylan Thomas and
Ransom, and maybe Yeats"—though I don't think
Yeats had ever cluttered me up. Much of what I'd been
reading was great stuff and a bit unfortunate for me. I
read Browning, and it occurred to me that I could
maybe write monologues, something I'd never at-
tempted before. So I wrote "Delta Farmer in a Wet
Summer," which is still a poem in anthologies. It
comes back. I think that was the first poem I ever wrote
that was mine, and I knew it. The day I wrote that
poem I knew that this was something, a way of working; this was a voice, strategy, technique, all those
funny words we use. Whatever, it seemed to be *my*
poem. "Delta Farmer" made a tremendous difference. I
had confidence in that poem.
Jones: And the other ones came quicker?
Whitehead: Much quicker. I throw away four
poems—maybe seven poems—for every one I keep. But
after that I began to write. After I got to Iowa, I wrote

rather rapidly, and then I had a year at Arkansas to do some new work. So I wrote *Domains* between—most of it must have been between '62 and '65, that whole book.

Jones: There's a poem in there called "At the Jackson Zoo, 1960."

Whitehead: That was written at Iowa City. In Iowa City I began to remember Mississippi. I was beginning to recollect that whole business of the lumber mills. I had time to write. I had more time to work than I'd had at Millsaps. I took time to work, at Millsaps, but that meant I'd get four hours' sleep. You can't write very well if you don't sleep. Sleeping is very important to writers. So I wrote most of the book in Iowa City. I wrote during the summer before we went up there and went at it fast and furiously after we were there.

Jones: Yes. You know, reading *Domains*—you said the civil rights movement was in full swing when you were writing most of the poems—I was struck by the fact that the poems show a contempt for bigots and the segregationist attitude that was evident in Mississippi during that time.

Whitehead: You know, I've never used the word bigot, I don't think. Civil liberties is a large and complicated issue, but it is something that, if we care about a democracy, we have to attend to in our imaginative and political lives.

Jones: Was Mississippi something that you felt you had to get away from?

Whitehead: Yes and no. I had to go back to school and I wanted to go to Iowa because Bill Harrison and Yount and others had been there. I needed time off. It seemed I'd go on being a college teacher, and I didn't want a Ph.D., so Iowa was the only place to go. I did not know that the Greensboro M.F.A. [Master of Fine Arts program] existed. I didn't want to go to Stanford, so I applied to Iowa. Those are the options I had. And, as I say, I had friends who'd gone there and liked it. I worked with Donald Justice and R. V. Cassill.

Jones: Donald Justice wrote one of my favorite poems, about driving through some small town at 3:00 A.M. and seeing one light on in the whole town, and "this poem is for whoever had the light on."

Whitehead: Yes, that's in "Night Light."

Jones: I told you I interviewed Walker Percy, and he said it's almost fatal for a writer to become overly concerned with social issues such as the civil rights movement. *Domains*, as I've heard you say, was written out of a sense of indignation—maybe that's too strong—at least a consciousness of what was going on in Mississippi at that time.

Whitehead: Well, the "domains" in there are love and politics. At least half the book is love poetry. I think about half of the book is love poetry mainly, and nature poetry. God help me, I did say that: "nature poetry." I don't know what Walker Percy's talking about. If you begin to believe in causes to the point where they turn human beings into caricatures and abstractions, then you're in jeopardy as an artist. But to believe passionately in rough justice and fair behavior and crude equity—it seems to me that that's not necessarily a damaging compulsion.

Jones: Yes, it's certainly part of life.

Whitehead: It sure as hell is part of his motivation as an artist. I think that what he would be saying is that the problem with causes very often will be the fact that people who get caught up in causes somehow believe that the cause will remove them from the responsibilities of their mortality. The fact is we are finite, mortal creatures, and all of our efforts for order and reason and decency will not go as far as we wish they would because we don't live long enough. In the human race each generation dies off and the next generation learns only a very little bit from the previous generation. History teaches us relatively little; although what it does teach us is terribly important. Science *seems* to go forward, while art—and faith—are always starting over. Thank God.

Jones: That's it.

Whitehead: Now, I don't know what he said, but he's a smart man.

Jones: You put it well.

Whitehead: He's a fine writer.

Jones: Yes. And your consciousness of the violence in the Mississippi character that ended in the killing of the three boys in Philadelphia still turns up in *Local Men*.

Whitehead: And the killing of Medgar Evers. He was a great man.

Jones: Yes. Did you ever meet him?

Whitehead: Yes, I talked to him a few times before he was shot. Those two conversations made a tremendous difference to me.

Jones: You met him during your time at Millsaps?

Whitehead: Yes, right.

Jones: At rallies?

Whitehead: No, it was out at the social science forum at Tougaloo.

Jones: At Ernst Borinski's.

Whitehead: At Ernst Borinski's, who was one of the most important people in my growing up. Absolutely. Borinski was tremendously important to the guys who were around here in the summers: Jim Miley, Gene Morrison, Tom McNair. The social science forum made a great deal of difference, and meeting Evers made a difference to me. I was ripe to have a hero at the time, and I don't think I was wrong to have had one. He [Medgar Evers] was one of the few absolutely confident men I've ever met, as well as being beautiful.

Jones: Absolutely confident?

Whitehead: He seemed to me at the time to be an extraordinarily confident man and spoke with great confidence about his inevitable death.

Jones: You know, talking to people who knew him, I have this image of him as being really tired near the end, tired of suffering the weight of imminent death.
Whitehead: Well, my recollection is probably skewed. There were two evenings I was with him. Two? I'm sure it was twice. He didn't seem tired, he seemed vivid to me. He spoke of his death, and he died within two weeks of the second time I spoke with him. I was in the kitchen on Marshall Street when the report came.
Jones: June 12, 1963.
Whitehead: Okay. That was the summer before I went to Iowa in September. Obviously, probably his death and all of that fired off lots of things in me after that.
Jones: And you talked about his death?
Whitehead: I did not. I was in a group of people as you would be, in the back room there talking. He made a talk one night. He talked of death while talking to all of us. One time a man from the East came down, a nice sociologist, and sort of made an antipopulist talk about how there was always going to be a total division of the races in the South. It was an erudite sort of wrong-headed presentation. I don't remember the man's name; he was white. And Evers stood up afterwards in the discussion and took him to task very gently and very thoroughly, and pointed out that's not what we were after, and that the whole struggle was to create a South in which black people and white people actually lived together as part of the same community, which, of course, we do not do to this very day.
Jones: And won't for the next few years.
Whitehead: We may be driven closer to that realization by the next four years.
Jones: Yes. My mother always told me about going out to Ernst's house for the social science forums.
Whitehead: I'm sure your mom and I went out there

together on occasion. I was so harried by being a husband who didn't know how to be a husband and a
father who didn't know how to be a father and a teacher
who didn't know how to be a teacher and a writer who
didn't know how to be a writer, and it was all going on
at the same time. Lord knows Gen did not divorce me
during that period of time probably because she was
raised Catholic. Thank God for that. I have pure, particular recollections, but my sense of time is totally off
base. I have a terrible time remembering. You dated
Medgar's death. I couldn't have given you that date for
the life of me, but I remember the kitchen, the orange
juice, the radio. We were making raisin wine in crocks
in the cupboard. I could not have remembered the day
to save me.

Jones: That must have been an interesting time to be
alive. As I was saying, even in *Local Men* you have a
couple of poems about Neshoba County men and being
at the Neshoba County Fair in '71 and feeling all those
old fears {"Trying to Explain a Bad Man to a Good Man
at the Neshoba County Fair 1971"]. That's a good
poem. Even as late as the '70s after the effects of the
civil rights movement had been felt, there's that
awareness of violence.

Whitehead: When were the killings in Neshoba
County?

Jones: June 21, 1964.

Whitehead: When did they make the arrests?

Jones: Late in the year, or perhaps January of '65.

Whitehead: No, it had to be February. It was later
on.

Jones: Oh, yes, a good while later.

Whitehead: Okay. We were coming home for spring
vacation. There was a blizzard going on in Iowa. I had
Gen and Bruun, who was a little fellow; Kat, who was
born in Jackson; and we had had Eric by that time. He
was just a bitty baby. He was born right after we got to

Iowa. We drove out of the blizzard, and by the time we got to Yazoo County, the sun came up: flowers and the spring. Well, they had just made the arrests, I believe, the way it turned out, and things were very touchy, very touchy. I came through, I believe it was Clarksdale, and we were trying to decide whether it would be better to go over to Highway 61 and come down or take 49 East. I laughed with Gen about it. I said, "We've got this Iowa tag on there and we'll sure as shooting get arrested." I drove out of town very slowly, and I was arrested.

Jones: In Clarksdale?

Whitehead: South of Clarksdale.

Jones: Bad place to be arrested.

Whitehead: And I got out of the car. Two dudes came up to me, and they couldn't see that I wasn't alone. Gen and the children were asleep in the car. The law said, "What are doing?" I said, "I am going to Yazoo City to visit my in-laws." They said, "Oh yeah?" Gen popped up in the seat about that time and was looking around, and they said, "Let me see your license," and I did all that. I had a Mississippi commercial driver's license at the time, and they said, "Why do you have a Mississippi commercial license and an Iowa tag?" So I said, "That's the way it works; if you've got your car in Iowa you got to have an Iowa tag, but you keep your Mississippi license." And he said, "Uh huh." By this time the heat was pretty well off, and I said, "Well, you arrested me on account of my tag, didn't you?" He said, "Oh, no, not really," the basic communication being that that was precisely what he'd done, and I said, "Oh, well, lot of trouble around, isn't there?" He said, "Oh, yeah," and he mentioned the arrests at the time. I said, "Listen, why'd you stop me? I wasn't speeding. I know what the speed limit is, and the city limits sign—I am out of the city limits. This is well beyond the city limits of Clarksdale." He said, "No,

you got that wrong." He said, "That sign is wrong
because that meant that the city limits is *way back there*
if you're coming *into* town, but *going out of town* the city
limits is *way down there.*" He pointed away into the
dark. That's a true story. I looked at him and said,
"Am I going to be arrested again between here and
Yazoo City?" He said, "There's a very good chance you
will be."

Jones: Especially if you went through Greenwood.

Whitehead: That was the next town. I said, "Okay,
I'm going to get arrested in Greenwood; give me your
name so I can at least tell them I know you." And I
wrote it down. I remember we smoked a Camel
cigarette there, leaning on the hood of my car.

Jones: With the policeman.

Whitehead: Two policemen, two sheriff's deputies or
whatever. I don't know what they were. We went on
and I did not get stopped anywhere between there and
Yazoo City. Gen, whose memory is perfect, would say
that's about right.

Jones: I like that story.

Whitehead: "The city limits is way down there, but
on this side it's way back there." You know, the city of
Clarksdale may be set up some way so it does that. I
don't know.

Jones: From the time you wrote *Domains* in 1966 to
the publication of *Joiner* in '71, Mississippi underwent a
massive social change with integration of the public
schools.

Whitehead: They said.

Jones: Exactly. Well, certainly legally.

Whitehead: Well, in practice too. We certainly
changed the form, if not the substance.

Jones: Well, violence was no longer a daily part of
black people's lives. How did that affect your writing?

Whitehead: I don't think it had anything to do with
it. *Joiner* was an imagination, a dream, a book that was

about an earlier time. It is set in the early years of the troubles. Sonny graduates from high school in '59. He leaves Dallas shortly after the Kennedy assassination in '63. The book ends the summer of '65.

Jones: Right, when Sonny kills Foots Magee.

Whitehead: Right, that's the time sequence. He was born in 1940. One of the simpler things I did was make him be born in 1940, and that helps.

Jones: One more question about *Domains*: do the poems in *Domains* seem dated to you now?

Whitehead: First books of poems are often anthologies of influences, and I'm not sure whether it was Miller Williams who told this to me or not. I think it was. Some critic of his first book, which was a good book, *A Circle of Stone,* said the book tended to be an anthology of influences.

Jones: Yes.

Whitehead: One critic of *Domains*, which was treated kindly, said that there were poems that I'd written as a poet and poems that I had written as practice poems.

Jones: Yes, exercises.

Whitehead: Exercises. There's a lot of truth to that. I don't think that *Domains* is so much an anthology of influences, but there are exercise poems in the book. I don't think, for example, that "Delta Farmer" and poems of that kind are really anybody else's poems but my own. But there are poems in there that are derivative and affected. Unfortunately, probably the most exercising poem in the book is the title poem. It has been anthologized and it is just as sneaky as can be and it makes all its little moves, and it is not a very good poem.

Jones: You would write it differently today?

Whitehead: Oh, no. You can't say that, Johnny. There's no writing what you did then, today. No, I did that poem with the absolute faith that I was trying to do something well, but while I was sitting writing in the Nissen hut in Iowa City I knew I was showing off. Oh, and it was well received in workshop. The really good poems were not often well received. They were thought to be too blunt, they were too rough in meter and texture, and often called obscure. A curious criticism—because I don't write obscure poetry. They were obscure to my fellow poets from other parts of the country. There was a sense of flash in the title poem that everybody could see. I don't reject the poem; it's just not a very good poem. I did the best I could with it, but it was just a kind of title-poem poem.

Jones: Does "Delta Farmer" stand out as the poem from that book you're most proud of?

Whitehead: You know, I haven't looked at that book lately. I like "First Lecture." I like "For a Neighbor Child."

Jones: I especially like that.

Whitehead: I like "Sikeston." "Miracle Play," now that's a phony poem. That's a literary poem. Boy, did they love that! Whoo, they loved that poem! It had complicated, resonant textures, ironies, allusions. I liked a little poem called "Eden's Threat," which I wrote in Arkansas. "Politician's Pledge" is done in rhymes and couplets of all kinds. That was anthologized in Germany. I like "The Lawyer." Let me find the one I like best. I think the one I like best is right on the brink, right on the brink, called "McComb City, August, 1958." I like that poem. I still do. That's on the brink. Maybe it falls over. I still like this book. I didn't know what I know now about music in poetry, and it will be interesting to see what I do with *Domains*, Lord willing, if I ever do a selected or collected poems, because I will be very tempted to revise the meters in several of these poems. They were rough and I like rough meters, but they are not as well controlled as I would have them be.

Jones: What about the idea for "McComb City?"

Whitehead: I was driving back—I had been down to see Miller Williams when he was—where in the hell was he? Sometime when he was at L.S.U. It must have been in the '60s. I'd gone to Baton Rouge and come back through McComb City and just had a sort of strange experience going through the town. And then somebody told me a story about being there in the '50s, in '58. I put my experience together with the story I was told by a friend. I dated the poem from the story, not the experience of actually being there. But then, of course, a story *is* an experience.

Jones: Mean city of bombings.

Whitehead: Yes. It's a complicated town because it was an old railroad town, wasn't it?

Jones: Yes, coming north from New Orleans toward Memphis.

Whitehead: Right. I don't have any animosity toward McComb; it's just my recollection of that one time and then somebody told me a story about it, and that's how it worked out.

Jones: Right. You were talking earlier about structure. In your poems you are a structuralist; you adhere to . . .

Whitehead: Formalist. Structuralism has gotten to mean something very different, as you surely know, in literary criticism. It's this new version of anthropological criticism, which means myth criticism, sociological structures, mental and phenomenological structures, the neo-Heideggerian literary criticism, which I'm very interested in. Heidegger is a great influence on me. I have a sneaking suspicion Percy has read Heidegger, too. I don't know it for sure, but I have this sneaking suspicion that he is a fellow Heidegger freak.

Jones: Heidegger, I think, was one of the first people to come up with the term "everydayness."

Whitehead: Well, it can be translated that way or as "the mundane." Everydayness is even better. I've pretty well read them through in the last ten years. Heidegger and Nietzsche. Well, what were we talking about?

Jones: We were talking about your not being a structuralist, but a formalist.

Whitehead: Right, form. Rhyme and meter, sir— iambic pentameter.

Jones: That's obviously very important to you.

Whitehead: Because it helps me write poems. The tension between the base metrical line and the prose expression focuses and amplifies everything that goes on in a poem. That's the main thing that separates a poem from prose, right?

Jones: Yes.

Whitehead: I've written free verse. I've committed free verse. An old friend of mine and a good critic of poetry called me—he's always wanting me to write recommendations for one grant or another—he called me the other night and he was going to review *Local Men* and he said, "Oh, that 'Troubled in a Dallas Hotel Room,' that's the kind of poetry you ought to be doing." That's my free verse poem. It enraged me! I like the poem, but it was a poem I considered something of a failure. I couldn't even get it in hexameters, let alone pentameters. Here he is praising this—it's better than I want it to be. The poem's really better than I wanted it to be.

Jones: "Hey, this is pretty good."

Whitehead: Right. No, I really wish that poem were not as much fun to people as it is. So I fussed at him, and then I said, "What a ridiculous thing to be doing, fussing at somebody for praising your free verse poem," but I did.

Jones: But it's something that you were able to do so well. Did that stuff really get going in the early '70s?

Whitehead: No, that stuff's been going on forever. We don't have tape or time enough to discuss where free verse is and formal verse is. You know, what is

King James English and *Samson Agonistes*, Milton's *Samson Agonistes?* It's some sort of Greek meter, understood the way Milton understood quantitative measure, and then an extension of English blank verse. Lord knows what it is! But it is great poetry. And rhythm is the more important concept in poetry than meter, but the way to a sort of rhythm I appreciate tends to be meter. Rhythm is the matter of concern, right?

Jones: Yes.

Whitehead: The way I get to rhythm is usually through meter. Meter is easier to memorize. It would be nice to write a memorable poem—also memorizable.

Jones: Do you make those stringent demands on yourself when you're writing prose?

Whitehead: I try to and I fail. Every now and then I'll stick one of my poems into a novel, break it up into prose. I did that a couple of weeks ago in *Coldstream*. I honestly can't remember which of the poems. Somewhere in *Joiner* is a section of one of the poems in *Domains*. I'm not sure which one it is right now, but it's in there. Very often in *Joiner* I take lines and images out of *Domains*, plagiarize them. *Domains* is greatly plagiarized in *Joiner*.

Jones: I never realized that.

Whitehead: Well, I wouldn't steal a whole stanza, but I'd just put in images. I think that's fair enough, don't you?

Jones: Sure, it's yours.

Whitehead: I got caught at it. One critic caught me, which I think is amazing because I didn't think anybody'd read *Domains*. I got an essay or something that said, "Whitehead has plagiarized himself."

Jones: I didn't know you could plagiarize yourself.

Whitehead: This was in good spirits and good fun.

Jones: I wanted you to tell me about the genesis of *Joiner*.

Whitehead: I wrote a short story in R. V. Cassill's

workshop in the spring of 1964. I love quoting these
dates with great confidence. It had to be '64. It could
not have been written in '65. They'd have thrown me
out if I hadn't written it by the spring of '64. It had to
be '64. It was called "What Went Wrong." It was
seventeen pages long. I read it once again in about
1970. It was about a character named Sonny Joiner who
was married to a girl named April, but I don't remember the story in detail.

Jones: Don't know what it was about?

Whitehead: Yes, I know what it was about. It was
about their divorce, but I don't remember what scenes
are in it.

Jones: Does Royal Carle play a part in it?

Whitehead: Yes.

Jones: In the short story.

Whitehead: Right. That's about as much as I remember. I remember it was well received. That was a marvelous bunch of men and women in that workshop: Joy
Williams; Diane Oliver, a marvelous black woman
who's dead now, killed in a motorcycle accident; Andre
Dubus; Mark Costello; Roger Rath, dead in an automobile accident; Ted Weeisner, one of the best writers
in the country; Kenneth Rosen, a poet and fiction
writer; Ann Mendell Eisenberg. Who am I leaving out?
Boy, it was phenomenal. There were maybe twenty
people in the workshop, and they've produced something like forty books. I thought all the workshops at
Iowa were like that, but I found out later that ours was
really a strange crowd.

Jones: Better than average.

Whitehead: Right. It was remarkable—a fluke, an absolute fluke. I haven't even begun to name the people
who were in there. Walt McDonald, who's at Lubbock
now. Anyway, that's where *Joiner* first showed up, in
the workshop.

Jones: What about that short story was memorable

enough that you wanted to sit down and work it into a novel?

Whitehead: I knew it was a rotten short story and so did Cassill, and he said, "This is obviously the beginning of a novel." I'd been told earlier by previous critics never to write about a football player.

Jones: Why?

Whitehead: I don't know. I never really believed it. Football was so traumatic to me, the loss of the game, that I hardly paid any attention to it at all for about five years. In fact I started going back and seeing football games in Iowa City; we lived right behind the stadium. When I wrote the story I said, "This is something to hand in for a class and it's fun." I was happy to be writing about football.

Jones: How long after you wrote the short story did you pick it back up to start *Joiner*?

Whitehead: I started almost immediately. I know I had written one hundred fifty pages by the time I went for interviews the next year—I was interviewed for a job at Emory and at Arkansas in the spring of '65. I'd written one hundred fifty pages, because I took those pages with me for my interviews at Emory and Arkansas.

Jones: Does that one hundred fifty pages now make up the first part of the book?

Whitehead: Whatever it was finally appeared in there in some form or another, but it was sketch work, cartooning. You know cartooning from painting?

Jones: Yes.

Whitehead: Well, that's what I had, the cartoon. That's what I've done over the last two years on *Coldstream*, the cartooning.

Jones: And it's not yet in a form where you're able to talk about it?

Whitehead: No.

Jones: How many drafts did *Joiner* take?

Whitehead: Four or five, I'm not sure how many there were. I know there were four.

Jones: And you thought as you produced each of them that that was the book that would be published?

Whitehead: No. In fact, there was some opinion rendered by the press that maybe the next-to-last draft was publishable, even though I had marginal comments on almost every page I sent in, every manuscript page. They seemed to think I was ready to publish it, but I took it back and worked on it for another year at least.

Jones: I've heard you say that the luckiest break of your life was getting the editor you got, Mr. Gottlieb?

Whitehead: Bob Gottlieb was very good to me. I hope he's good to me again. But if he isn't, somebody else may be. Maybe I'll run out of luck. It's harder to publish novels right now than it was when I sold *Joiner.*

Jones: Because of the competition?

Whitehead: No, the business end of it. I can handle the competition; I'm not sure I can handle the business. No, Bob was good to me. I was glad to sell it at the time. I needed money because Gen was about to have triplets. He bought it the day the first of the triplets came home from the hospital.

Jones: Good timing.

Whitehead: Yes, that added a little bit of money to the till.

Jones: And what form was the book in when you sold it?

Whitehead: It was one hundred fifty pages of chaos.

Jones: He bought that?

Whitehead: He bought that. That's why I said Padgett read those one hundred fifty pages and was a bit amazed that anybody in New York would take such a chance.

Jones: Just on the prospect that . . .

Whitehead: He paid very little money for it. Get that in perspective.

Jones: But on the prospect that in the near future you would produce the complete novel.

Whitehead: Yes.

Jones: And how long did that take?

Whitehead: Two years.

Jones: And four drafts?

Whitehead: Yes.

Jones: And did it consume totally your free time?

Whitehead: I don't know what free time is, John.

Jones: Time outside of your professional obligations.

Whitehead: It occupied a great deal of my time.

Jones: Was he on your back about getting the novel in?

Whitehead: No.

Jones: You were lucky, weren't you?

Whitehead: Well, he didn't have much invested in me. He could write me off for gum wrappers. He got him a pretty good book out of the deal. We made some money off of it, not too much, but a little. And he was very, very nice. It was great, a wonderful experience. I'd like to have it again.

Jones: Who else does he edit?

Whitehead: Oh, he's edited everybody, I guess. He's been Updike's editor, if he's not now. Cheever, Doris Lessing, Anthony Burgess, John Gardner. Those are the lesser writers he's been involved with.

Jones: Yes, the hacks. It must have been hard to find the voice for *Joiner*, a remarkable example of taking the way people communicate and using it in not only the dialogue but the narrative.

Whitehead: You've never heard that voice before?

Jones: Sure, I've heard the voice before, but I haven't
. . .

Whitehead: Where have you heard that voice before?

Jones: I grew up in Mississippi, and I . . .

Whitehead: You're a good listener.

Jones: Try to be.

Whitehead: All right. I try to be a good listener. There may be some of your father in that book.

Jones: I think so. Did it take an evolution of technique to come up with a voice that you were comfortable with?

Whitehead: I don't even know how to talk about that. I don't think anybody does. You fill yourself up with the books you read and you fill yourself up with the voices of the people you care about, and you hear your own voice; and if you're lucky and you have a story to tell, then all of it begins to hang together. At the center in the beginning of that book was the story of a guy who loses his wife. His best friend marries his true love. If you know anything about that experience, you must realize that in the midst of that experience there is a voice, and it's all the voices you hear while the pain is going on. Pain becomes marvelously articulate.

Jones: Pain?

Whitehead: Pain becomes greatly articulate, if you listen carefully.

Jones: People writing about *Joiner* say it's a wonderful language novel, takes Southernese to new heights. Is that what you were attempting to do? Was that in your mind?

Whitehead: It wasn't in my mind to take Southernese to new heights. Who would want to take Southernese to new heights? It sounds like taking a loose woman up in an elevator. Taking Southernese to new heights?

Jones: I'm afraid that's mine.

Whitehead: No, that's almost exactly what they said. No, I'm not picking on you. That is what has been said.

Jones: What's a language novel?

Whitehead: I don't know what a language novel is. Who writes language novels? Is Scott Fitzgerald a language novelist?

Jones: I wouldn't think so.

Whitehead: Well, I do. You don't think so? You can't memorize it?

Jones: Oh, yes . . .

Whitehead: You don't think Fitzgerald is lyric?

Jones: Yes. I was thinking mainly of the writers who take the way the language is spoken, mainly spoken, around them and make a new sound in their writing, like those Texas writers or even Miss Welty.

Whitehead: Well, she does that brilliantly. She does it beautifully again and again. The dialogue—oh, man, it's just gorgeous.

Jones: Yes.

Whitehead: Is Hemingway a language novelist?

Jones: Not in the sense that I mean.

Whitehead: Well, you know what they mean sometimes when they say language novelist? They mean bullshit. They mean that you've been rhetorical, Proustean, Joycean, Steinean, like that, Grassean. That means you're carrying on. Wolfean, the ultimate attack, the great writer. The original Thomas Wolfe. Little taught, little attention paid to him these days.

Jones: Yes, college professors like to say he's a novelist for young idealistic men.

Whitehead: Yes, that's a good way to dismiss a good writer.

Jones: You like him?

Whitehead: Right. I think he's not given his due. I haven't read him enough since I was a young man, and I confess that. I was thinking about rereading him and teaching him.

Jones: They attack his involuted, rambling style.

Whitehead: His carrying on.

Jones: And his being imprecise.

Whitehead: Well, I never thought of Wolfe as being terribly imprecise, and I certainly don't think of *Joiner* as being especially imprecise. Certainly not, though it is, on occasion.

Jones: What about the way you handle time in *Joiner?* You jump from here, the present, to the past, to the League.

Whitehead: Well, it's a foreground, background proposition. I read that in a critical work on the book—that it was foreground, background. It has to do with where he is when he starts telling the story, and then he goes back to, the critics say, "the proximate present." Does that make sense?

Jones: Yes.

Whitehead: But it seems to me that's the way we tell a story sometimes. "The Rime of the Ancient Mariner." He fixes you with his, what? "Glittering eye." Huh?

Jones: Yes.

Whitehead: And you are the "wedding guest." You cannot "but hear." You have to listen to the story. I wish the book were twenty-five pages shorter.

Jones: What would you cut out?

Whitehead: I don't know, but I know it's twenty-five pages too long. I'm not positive which twenty-five it is.

Jones: Did you cut *Joiner?*

Whitehead: Thirteen pages.

Jones: In what area? Do you mind telling me this?

Whitehead: No, I don't mind telling you. The most interesting thing is that Bob, who's a superb and wonderful editor, wanted to cut out the tree people, which would have been a mistake—since it's the central action of the novel. And he is a marvelous editor. I mean that. He misunderstood what was happening at that point. But there was also a chapter where six psychiatrists in a white Cadillac appeared to psychoanalyze Maylene Smith, which was digressive, irrelevant, outrageous, and totally disjunct. But I left it in, and Bob cried out in his living room in New York, "This must go!" I said, "I think you're right!" I must find that in a drawer somewhere. I love that scene. They appeared, driving over the hills, these psychiatrists in a white Cadillac.

Jones: Is this before she goes out to where the buzzard's been hit by lightning?

Whitehead: Yes, yes. I don't know. I had a great time writing the scene. It was right in there. It couldn't have happened! Right?

Jones: Right, in Bryan, Mississippi.

Whitehead: No, there was no way. It was a good scene, but it didn't work.

Jones: Gottlieb didn't want you to take anything else out?

Whitehead: Oh, yes, he would have; he would have made the book much, much shorter, I think.

Jones: And you disagreed with him?

Whitehead: Yes, I disagreed with him. Either I was right or didn't know better.

Jones: I've heard that criticism before of *Joiner*, that it could stand to be a little shorter, but I could never think what it could do without.

Whitehead: Well, you're sweet to say that. I don't know either. I told you all I know about cutting it. I felt like it was done when it was done, so I let it go. Then I wrote the last four or five pages in New York on the floor of an office at Knopf.

Jones: On the floor?

Whitehead: Yes. That was nice. I had it ending with a letter. It doesn't end with a letter now.

Jones: No, he's driving back home.

Whitehead: Yes. They do the thing at the courthouse. But I had another ending when I carried it to New York. That whole courthouse section, and then going out on the road, was done in New York. I brought it to New York and I said, "I don't like the end," and Bob said, "I don't either," and so I said, "Look, I've got three days. I'll come up here and work. I'll bring my legal pad and my pencil up here and work on it until I get it right, these last few pages."

Jones: And did you have the courthouse scene written?

Whitehead: Yes, some of it. Let me see the book. I want to show you where I picked up on the seventeenth floor. This is a book I haven't reread either. I'm going to have to reread it. I wrote from here, see there?

Jones: Yes.

Whitehead: I wrote from here to the end.

Jones: Three pages.

Whitehead: Well, on a legal pad that would be, one, two, three, about seven pages on a legal pad. I worked in the Knopf offices for two or three mornings. I was on the floor in an office of a guy who was out of town. It was a beautiful place with a view of the river and everywhere. It was a small office and to stretch out I had to leave the door open. The desk was uncomfortable so I was stretched out there writing on a legal pad and throwing things over in the corner. There were people who would walk by and look in and say, "Who are you?" I would say, "I'm not Mr. So-and-so because he's on leave." "What are you doing?" I said, "I'm finishing a novel," and they would look at me rather oddly. So at the end of either the second or third morning I took the legal pad down to Bob and read it aloud to him, and he said, "That's good. That's the way it ought to end," and he typed it up for me in the office.

Jones: Well, if I remember right, the last three pages has the local J.P. decide not to bind Joiner over to the grand jury, and telling him to leave Bryan.

Whitehead: Yes, I had that in the letter. What I finally did was just tell it straight out.

Jones: Well, that's a good insight into what goes into writing a novel.

Whitehead: I don't think it's a good insight into writing novels. I don't think it has anything at all to do with novels *in general.* It was a very peculiar and delightful . . . I was very pleased that that happened. I had no idea it was going to happen.

Jones: Well, let me ask you this: in the criticism of

Joiner there's a considerable discussion of how you bring in bits and pieces of the Bohemian Revolution and the history of the English Levellers. Is that supposed to be reflective of Sonny's own view of his predicament?

Whitehead: Yes, sure. He's a college kid and he reads Winstanley and Abiezer Coppe and Hus and reads about Zizka and Procop, and he's aware that there's some kind of revolution going on in *his* time, and he thinks of his own condition as a yeoman farmer's son, or as a mill worker's son, a mechanic's son—a mechanic in the sense that a mechanic is a mechanic in a lumber mill—and tries to tie the things together. Of course, they don't really fit. They are spiritually related, but the civil rights movement that he was dealing with was far from being exactly like the Levellers. But both were populist revolutions! A lot of work has been done on Winstanley and the Levellers.

Jones: Relating it to the social movements of the '60s, yes.

Whitehead: Yes, it became popular, was rediscovered. I found that material in an anthology called *Revolution: European Radicals from Hus to Lenin,* edited by a man whose name is Charles H. George.

Jones: And reading that you thought it was appropriate for Sonny.

Whitehead: I lucked into it. I'd written a draft and a half of the book, and I knew something was missing, and I sat down one night and started reading long excerpts from Winstanley and Coppe, and I said, "My God, this is what Sonny has been getting in college." The sections from J. F. H. Claiborne are from the great Claiborne *Mississipi, as a Province, Territory and State,* which was a book given to me by Charles East—Lord, I don't know when this was. I had poems accepted for *Southern Writing in the Sixties.* When did that come out? '65, '66. [1966–67] I went to Baton Rouge; I was there with Miller, and Charles East gave me my copy of

Mississippi, as Province, Territory and State by Claiborne, and I read it. I knew that would finally be somewhere in the book. Now, you talk about a book that's written in Faulknerian prose and Carlylian prose and that marvelous nineteenth century rhetoric! There are some of the finest Faulknerian passages in Claiborne you can imagine. I do not recollect in any Faulkner biography there being a mention that Faulkner read Claiborne, but I bet he did. Do you know Claiborne?

Jones: Yes. The Department published Claiborne's book, and we have his papers at the Archives.

Whitehead: Sure. Well, that's a great, great book. *Joiner* is pretty well loaded up with some of that. A lot of the prose that I was working with is playing with the idea of talking Smith County redneck mixed with Winstanleyan. British Leveller talk wrapped up in Claiborne on certain occasions. I actually had that in mind every now and then.

Jones: Does this fit in with what we were talking about earlier, this Southerner's burden of history?

Whitehead: We may have a greater burden of history, but I don't think we're necessarily more concerned with our history than other places. Iowa is tremendously concerned. Arkansas is a great Southern state, and it has almost no sense of its own history. One of the things we're trying to do now in Arkansas is collect the last hundred years of history of the state of Arkansas. It has not been collected! Willard Gatewood, a fine Southern historian, has the chair at Arkansas, and he is trying to collect the history. Arkansans have not collected their history! They've paid very little attention to it. People like my grandmother—they really need to interview her, because they have not done well in collecting history.

Jones: Yes. For instance, I didn't know about the Union sympathizers in Arkansas.

Whitehead: Oh, all the Ozarks were Union for the most part. The Confederate Arkansans came to Fayette-

ville and Pea Ridge to fight the Union Arkansans. You
can get that in Shelby Foote. Slavery declines with
every foot of rise above sea level.

Jones: Same thing in east Tennessee.

Whitehead: Absolutely the same. Well, nothing's absolutely the same, but it's essentially the same thing.
You don't have mountain blacks, nobody had planta-
tions, you didn't have slave labor. Just as the Free State
of Jones [Jones County, Mississippi] seceded from the
Confederacy, insofar as it seceded, because they were
not slave owners, though not far above sea level.

Jones: Yes, we're not going to fight a rich man's battle
with poor men.

Whitehead: It has been done several times, hasn't it?

Jones: Yes. Tell me about the concept of the natural
man as you used it in *Joiner* and in *Local Men*. The
natural man would smoke, would light up another
Picayune. Do you know what I am talking about?

Whitehead: That's meant to be, I hope, somewhat
true, and also in fun. A natural person has fun. *Joiner* is
a comic novel basically. It isn't always funny, but it is
basically a comic novel in the larger sense of comic,
sure.

Jones: And having this six-foot-seven . . .

Whitehead: No, that's not hyperbole at all. There're a
lot of tackles who're much taller. He was six-nine originally, and Gottlieb cut him down to six-seven, which I
let him do. But, you know, I've known professional
tackles who are six-eight, six-nine.

Jones: But in what sense do you mean comic novel?

Whitehead: The main character survived. It's based on
an irony that's essentially affirmative. It starts on a
down swing and ends in an affirmation. The voice of
the book is a voice of celebration. And I hope it's funny
once in a while.

Jones: It is. Ends in an affirmation? I thought he was
on his way back to stop Royal and April.

Whitehead: No, he's just on his way back home with

his new woman. It starts down and ends up. It's comedy in the sense of Christian comedy, or Western post-Greek comedy.

Jones: And the natural man?

Whitehead: I don't remember anything in there about a natural man.

Jones: Sure. The natural man should enjoy every physical pleasure, you know, as well as intellectual.

Whitehead: Well, that's when he's talking about Royal Carle. I think you're talking about Sonny saying that Royal was strung out and self-conscious and wouldn't do all these things that the rest of the boys would do when they were growing up. Royal was a little inhibited, and still is. Have I made a case for the natural man? I don't know really what a natural man is, exactly, though I do think I understand, in the Wordsworthian sense, what natural piety is: reverence for nature, and I do think I know that people who're in contact with themselves physically are better off than those who aren't. Sonny is not alienated from his body. He is struggling between angelism and bestialism maybe, but he's not having a hell of a lot of trouble. Sonny's problem is that he's ignorant.

Jones: In a way that Royal isn't?

Whitehead: Well, they're both ignorant. My God, the book ends when the boys are twenty-five years old! Sonny's only twenty-five years old when the book ends!

Jones: Yes, that's pretty ignorant.

Whitehead: Did I tell you about the lady who wrote me a letter and said she liked the book but berated me about Sonny being promiscuous? Well, I thought it was wonderful that he was accused of promiscuity. I read the letter and felt the assault and was set back by it, discouraged by it, but I accepted the praise and began to think. Then I began to laugh after I realized how silly it was.

Jones: I thought he was pretty promiscuous.

Whitehead: Not at all. Not at all! All right, it ends when he is twenty-five years old, right?

Jones: Yes.

Whitehead: How many women has he had?

Jones: Four.

Whitehead: Four! Now how in the world is that promiscuity? How many Mississippi men of his generation, coming out of the world at the age of twenty-five, having gone through all of college football, and professional football for at least part of the season, have slept with only four women? One was his wife. Most of the love scenes are between Sonny and his wife, right?

Jones: But still, he speaks of women like someone who is promiscuous.

Whitehead: Promiscuity is when you have many frivolous relationships, when you go through many people thoughtlessly, and when those relationships are merely carnal. He's not promiscuous in any way, shape, or form! Look it up in the dictionary!

Jones: Okay. Well, his thought is certainly promiscuous.

Whitehead: His thought is not promiscuous. His thought is sensual.

Jones: Would you say that he [Sonny] is not lewd in his references to women and such?

Whitehead: Lewd is a marvelously old-fashioned word. I don't mind him being lewd.

Jones: Walker Percy uses it a lot.

Whitehead: Walker Percy works with great skill and vision from a different perception of society than I do.

Jones: Yes.

Whitehead: He writes about rich people.

Jones: Right. But you remember in *The Last Gentleman* he talks about Sutter Vaught saying that the only pure thing left in society these days . . .

Whitehead: Is lewdness. Yes, you know, I might say

raunchiness and I like the word *carnal*, but I don't think that's the only thing left. Sonny is a secret Christian.

Jones: There was some criticism of *Joiner* that the language was too rough, not at all the language of a Christian in the traditional sense.

Whitehead: Well, that's only a particular. That's a recent aberration in the faith. He's physical. He's not disjunct from his body. But I think Sonny is essentially a Christian. I really didn't realize that until I wrote the scene in which he said it. Until I wrote the scene I didn't realize that that's what he was, even though he tears down Billy Graham's pulpit. He considers Graham's religion a Gnosticism, as opposed to genuine Christianity.

Jones: You're talking about the scene when he cries out in a rage that Billy Graham Christianity isn't what it is all about.

Whitehead: I replay that scene—that is one of the scenes I replay in the new book.

Jones: Back to lewdness. Does Sonny say the same thing to himself that Sutter Vaught says, that lewdness is all we have?

Whitehead: No, he doesn't make those distinctions. That's not his problem. I don't know whether he's deep or broad or what, but he isn't suffering a disjunction; he's not suffering alienation. *Coldstream* is alienated. You want alienation from me, you're about to get four or five hundred pages of alienation, God help me. I didn't think I'd ever do it, but it's on me. Royal is alienated, badly alienated. I guess we can use that word, can't we? I guess we have to use that word.

Jones: It's a basic condition.

Whitehead: No, but we have to tease it, laugh at it.

Jones: But Sonny wasn't that disjointed?

Whitehead: He was getting disjointed by other things. He was getting disjointed by the fact that he suddenly realized that there was a difference between being black and white, and having a woman and not. He loses his career, he loses his . . . he thought he was a football player, and it turns out he is both a football player and a neophyte intellectual. He loses his game and he loses his lover. Okay?

Jones: Okay. Well, I liked Sonny all the way through the novel.

Whitehead: Oh, I didn't like him all the way through. I don't dislike him. But I don't approve of him entirely.

Jones: I especially didn't approve of his treatment of April at the end when he was so brutal to her.

Whitehead: Oh, yes. He's a fool. He's a meathead.

Jones: What else did he do that you didn't like through the novel?

Whitehead: I think it's something that we all know, at least some of us do—that is if you are spoiled—you know, he's an only child, and if you're given everything that your particular little tribe has to give and you're on top of the heap in your little tribe, you are often insensitive to the pains of others. Consequently, a lot of his good high spirits, when he recollects himself, presents himself as a young man, is high spirits in the midst of something he simply doesn't understand. Had he not lost his wife, had he not become a fool, he would have become a frivolous man.

Jones: Was it hard when you were writing about Sonny to separate yourself, Jim Whitehead, from Sonny Joiner? Could you cut the faucet off?

Whitehead: No, I didn't cut it off very well at all. I ceased to be me to a great extent and became him.

Jones: Is that just part of the creative process?

Whitehead: I don't think you can generalize about that. When you are talking to writers, when you're talking to doctors or lawyers, everybody goes about their business a hundred different ways.

Jones: Yes. About that phone booth we talked about

earlier, he says, "the metaphysics of claustrophobia may finally be the sum of what a large man's book is all about." Remember?

Whitehead: Yes.

Jones: Would you tell me something of what you were thinking about when you wrote that line?

Whitehead: I think I know what it means. To be as large as Sonny is is to be constantly observed. To be an athlete is to be constantly observed. To be an athlete in a sport in which you're filmed and reviewed on film, every physical act that you commit in your trade reviewed and criticized meticulously and graded, and to have gone through that experience through four years of high school, four years of college, and then pro ball, is a kind of nightmare. It is, in fact, what they taught us in church was Judgment Day. It was that your life would be replayed for you before God, and all the sins that you've committed and every act and nastiness and perversion and confusion. You'd have to look at it again. Of course, the Christian story is that if you accept Christ then you'll never have to look at that movie in the future. You'll never have to have your life replayed. So Sonny really wants to avoid God's game movie. I think the greater vision is the one in which you could stand to see it all played again, to watch that movie. I don't know what it would do to you. It would shame me and horrify me. I'm not strong enough to stand it. I don't think it's the case, of course. I think maybe the better person would be the one who would say, "Yes, all right, let's see that again. I can stand it. Not only will I see it again, I'll do it again," which is, of course, Nietzsche's concept of the eternal return, which he writes about most eloquently not in *Zarathustra* but in *Ecce Homo,* a late work. In other words, Nietzsche says he would not change anything backward or forward, not through all eternity—not only affirm it, but love it! That is asking a great deal of us. Probably too much. Does that make sense?

Jones: Certainly does.

Whitehead: Well, you asked about that business of claustrophobia. It's because he's under scrutiny.

Jones: Yes, under the only light in the darkness.

Whitehead: Yes, right. One of the things I liked about working on *Local Men* was that I was living with people who were really a long way off from *Joiner*. Whew, what a relief. And with adults. *Local Men* is a book mostly about adults.

Jones: Yes. Has your style changed from *Joiner* to your present writing on *Coldstream*?

Whitehead: Yes, it's changed a good deal, really.

Jones: I promised you we wouldn't talk about it, so I'll keep my promise. But you started off writing a book called "Boykin."

Whitehead: Yes, and it didn't work. I wrote many pages of that book. It simply didn't take. I did a lot of research on it. I spent a lot of time in chancery court, went to trials. It wasn't his book. It really wasn't.

Jones: How long?

Whitehead: Two and a half years probably.

Jones: Gosh. Do you hope to eventually return to it?

Whitehead: I have no idea. Man, just let me get through this one, and then I'll worry about the next one. Truly.

Jones: Yes.

Whitehead: "Boykin" is *Local Men*. That's the God's truth. What happened was I couldn't write that novel, but the lawyers and sheriffs and all the people I listened to while I was—thought I was—writing a novel turned into that book of poems.

Jones: Well, you came up with something quite remarkable with that research.

Whitehead: It was research of the most casual order. But patient, I'll say that for it. I owe a great deal to my friend Tom Royals, of course, for taking me to court and tolerating all my questions. Tom will tend on occasion to claim that 99 percent of what I write is taken directly from his stories and his life. This is not entirely true.

Jones: As you say in *Local Men*: "All I say is that it isn't possible."

Whitehead: In "Pay Attention, Son."

Jones: I like that poem.

Whitehead: That's funny too. That poem ended up in some anthology or textbook lately. I have always been surprised by that poem.

Jones: Thought it was an inside joke?

Whitehead: No, it's not really an inside joke or poem. I'm pleased that somebody likes it. It's not free verse, but it's a fairly loose poem.

Jones: Let me ask you, Jim, how the poetic impulse differs from the impulse to write prose.

Whitehead: You're working with different controls. Poetry relies on the line as the basic unit of control. I actually gave what I think is a very good definition of the line in poetry when I was talking at that meeting here last month. I can't remember exactly what I said. Essentially, in prose the line runs to the end of the page and then turns around arbitrarily, right?

Jones: Yes.

Whitehead: There's nothing arbitrary about the length of the line in a poem, right? It makes all the difference in the world. It is a musical unit of composition, and a rhetorical and grammatical unit of composition. Syntax in poetry is under a kind of pressure that is more abstract and more exactly formal than prose is. That's not to say that prose isn't full of marvelous variations and rhythms and possibilities. We all work hard to give it that sort of expressive, rhetorical quality. Maybe poetry's simpler. The way I write a poem, most of it will have ten syllables, ten to twelve syllables per line, it will rhyme more often than not, and it will be somewhere between fourteen and one hundred fifty lines long. This is a great relief. You are simply bound to one obligation, which is to make no mistakes.

Jones: Every word counts.

Whitehead: It all has to work. One hopes that it will work from beginning to end. Mr. Frost said, "I write poems in order to see if I can get to the end of them," or "to the end of it." That's about right.

Jones: Another famous story about Frost is the time the lady asked him, "You really don't think about all the structural and formal elements when you sit down to write a poem, do you?"

Whitehead: "I revel in them." That's great. That may be one of the most famous lines in modern criticism. It's the justification for all formal poetry maybe, lately.

Jones: But when you sit down to write, are you aware of a whole different frame of mind that conceives poetry and prose?

Whitehead: Oh, sure. You know you're involved in a very different activity. You're not dealing with a long scene and you're not connecting it with thirty pages before and one hundred fifty pages after, and you're not dealing with dialogue in the way the dialogue is related in a narrative. All of that. It's radically different. Oh, how to express it. You can visualize a poem. When you finish a poem, you can pin it up on your wall, get it on a blackboard and write it all out, you can memorize it, and that may be the most important thing. You can recite it to yourself and therein correct your mistakes. You can read it aloud and recite it to other people, and they can hear the flaws in it. All manner of things make it other than writing fiction. It's a great relief. The ones you lose are the troublesome ones. In my case, a curious experience—I hate to tell this story because I'm afraid it reinforces bad habits—but I will sit down and think I am going to write poem A, and I'll write for days— two, three, four days on poem A—and then by some curious process of deflection, poem B will come from poem A, and it may or may not have anything to do with the poem I thought I was going to write. It's curious. I will sit down and believe that poem A is what I'm doing and work on it with complete diligence. Once in a while I'll actually finish poem A, but most often after three days of slaving over poem A, I write poem B relatively quickly. And it didn't necessarily have anything to do with the one I worked on for three days.

Jones: That's interesting. You just have the poetic structure in your mind . . .

Whitehead: That's not a structure; that's a bad habit. That's something that's going on that I wish did not go on. I'm wasting a lot of time. I have literally hundreds of poem A's stuck off in a corner of my study, and they've all got nice lines and jogs and rhythms in them. I find them on legal pads years later and I read them— really strange.

Jones: But you're thinking poem.

Whitehead: I know I've got a poem in me. That much I'm sure of. But you think it's one thing and then it turns into another. I was scrubbing around looking for something in my study the other day and found a section of *Joiner* written out as a poem. There it was. It must have been written in '66, '67. My handwriting has changed since then. So I knew it must have been early because my handwriting changed somewhere around '69.

Jones: A poem about April?

Whitehead: No, it was a descriptive passage. It could've been the bridge; it could've been anything. It was something that got incorporated later in *Joiner*. That deflection is the curious experience, and I would like to break that habit. Days when I write poetry I have a lot of exercises I do. I've written dozens of sestinas and I've only published one. I've written fifty villanelles and I've never finished one. I almost had one once.

Jones: "Sestina With a Long Last Line," is that it?

Whitehead: That's the only one I've ever finished.

Jones: What is it? "The Narrative Hooper and
L.D.O."
Whitehead: "Sestina With a Long Last Line."
Jones: A great poem.
Whitehead: That's a popular poem, that's a pop
poem. I like that poem okay, but that poem will
plague me. It will be anthologized when many of my
favorite children are left in obscurity.
Jones: "I'm no hooper—I'm from Dumas, Arkansas."
Whitehead: I have wanted to say that the experience
of travelling with Tom T. Hall was very important to
me, and my awkward and sometimes troubled friendship with him has been useful. I'm not name dropping.
He's a very fine writer. He has a novel coming out next
year with Doubleday. Maybe he's a genius. And we
don't get along very well a lot of the time, but twice
this summer we were back together and had a really
good time. The year that I travelled with him off and
on was a wonderful experience. Six or seven poems in
Local Men are about that time.
Jones: Yes.
Whitehead: And there's a large country music section
in *Coldstream*. Tom's a superb artist and one of the most
extraordinary people I've ever been privileged to know.
Jones: I've never thought or heard he was a genius.
Whitehead: That's because you've never heard the
songs that were not on the charts. See, you need to get
the records and listen to the story songs. Oh, they are
wonderful songs.
Jones: What year did you travel with Tom T.?
Whitehead: I'm not sure. It must have been sum-
mer—it was either the summer of '72 or the summer of
'73. I think it was '73.
Jones: Doing research for "Boykin?"
Whitehead: No, I was running off.
Jones: Oh, I see.
Whitehead: "Boykin" had gone smash, I was driving

Gen crazy, and all that. I met Tom T. here in Jackson and went off to Fort Worth the first time with him. We swarmed in Fort Worth at Panther Hall. It was something I was interested in, and I needed to shake the tree. That's what shook the tree. It did it! It probably had as much to do with my finishing *Local Men* as anything. Glenn Ray was Tom T.'s steel man at the time. That's the reason I dedicated it to him. When Tom and I were not getting along too well, Glenn would tell Tom not to throw me off the bus.

Jones: What about the poem in there where he fires a hot lead guitar player?

Whitehead: Yes, that's an interpolation of a true story. It's much fictionalized. It should've been dedicated to Pete Blue, but I never could find Pete to show the poem to him. I think Pete would like it. Sometime I'll find Pete and show it to him.

Jones: Did you travel around in Hall's big bus?

Whitehead: Yes. I carried the musical instruments. It was enlightening, elevating, and humiliating. Not many people have run off with a country band while they were on a Guggenheim.

Jones: And you just stayed with him for that summer.

Whitehead: Off and on.

Jones: I knew that you were close to him.

Whitehead: Near and far.

Jones: Yes.

Whitehead: He's really much closer to Miller than he is to me. Miller gets along with him much more easily than I do, though Tom and I are learning to get along.

Jones: Let me ask you this: in the epigraph of *Local Men* you quote Malatesta . . .

Whitehead: Errico Malatesta. He was an Italian anarchist, a rich man, sort of a socialist St. Francis of Assisi. And he wrote the great essay called "Anarchy." Or "Anarchism," I can't remember.

Jones: Nineteenth century revolutionary?

Whitehead: Twentieth.

Jones: He talks about the metaphysical tendency in academia which confuses abstraction with the real thing.

Whitehead: Not in academia. That's never mentioned.

Jones: I guess that's what I'm asking; it seems especially true in academia.

Whitehead: That happens no more in academia than anywhere else. "There is a disease of the human mind called the metaphysical tendency, that causes man, after he has by logical process abstracted the quality from an object, to be subject to a kind of hallucination that makes him take the abstraction for the real thing. . ." [quoting Malatesta from epigraph of *Local Men*]. That's about half playful. What's the real thing?

Jones: Well, let me ask you about the idea of combining academics and creativity.

Whitehead: The usual question is "Have you lost any books because you are a school teacher?" The answer is sure, sure I've lost five years of my career as a writer because I've been a school teacher. But I'm also a school teacher, and that's one of the arts I'm interested in. I write poetry and I try to write novels on occasion, and I practice the art of school teaching.

Jones: Can you teach someone creative writing?

Whitehead: You can't teach anyone creativity. You can teach people how to write better. You can help their work by editing it.

Jones: Some writers have told me that the worst place for a working writer to be is on a college campus.

Whitehead: That's interesting. How many of them have not been on college campuses?

Jones: Some have been on campuses less than others. I get this bias from Shelby Foote.

Whitehead: Shelby is rich, too. And he is an important writer. His narrative history of the Civil War is a joy and a wonder.

Jones: What he said was that during the tough time of

the '30s that the great writers—Faulkner, Hemingway, Fitzgerald—were not teaching but writing and perfecting their craft.

Whitehead: I understand that. But still I believe in teaching. There's a great deal to be said for the other way of going—and I suppose I will always wonder what I would have done had I not stayed married and committed myself to trying to be a father of some kind or another to seven children. But that is what I do, and I love it, so that's not a useful problem for me.

Jones: I certainly didn't mean to challenge that.

Whitehead: No, it comes up and it's a necessary question to ask. There aren't too many cases in the history of letters, arts and letters, of people who have been married and raised families. It's a kind of repudiation of married life and family raising. Somehow the artist is supposed to be the adversary of marriage and the family. I am absolutely the opposite. I am the advocate of marriage and the family. Bruun, Kathleen, Eric, Joan, Philip, Edward, Ruth! I'm hostile to divorce, and I don't believe we are supposed to thin ourselves out and give up breeding. In that way I'm a rank conservative, I suppose. To hell with it.

Jones: So editing and reading others' work does sap your creative instinct?

Whitehead: Sometimes. And teaching is an ephemeral art form. It's very much like serious acting. Maybe teaching is the most existential of all art forms.

Jones: How?

Whitehead: Because it's gone!

Jones: Well, Jim, we really have talked for three hours.

Whitehead: We really have.

Jones: Let me say how much I appreciate it.

Photograph Courtesy of Dorothy Cassity

Turner Cassity

June 4, 1980

I'd missed the lecture Mr. Cassity gave at Millsaps
College in the spring of 1980. There he ruffled a few
feathers by elaborating on some of the same sentiments
he expresses in this interview: that the old tradition is
dead, and the Southern novelists from Faulkner to the
present are of little value to him as a writer. An interview with him promised to be interesting, if a bit
difficult. His art reveals little of the man himself, but
shows a formalist who believes that language in the
poetic structure is sufficient and that personal revelation
is unnecessary. And it seemed to me that the "vanishing poet" was dealing no less authentically with the
world in his work than other writers, except that it was
not exclusively the world of his native South. We
agreed to meet early on a June morning, and I was
watching for him as he pulled into the Archives park-
ing lot in a car packed to the roof with luggage. He
was driving from Atlanta to Palo Alto, California, to
spend eight weeks typing and revising a year's produc-
tion of his poetry. I greeted a small man at the door—
wearing glasses and sporting a real crew cut—and we
sat and talked for an hour in the Archives meeting
room under the blank stares of two busts of George

Washington and Robert E. Lee. Then the "vanishing poet" vanished.

Jones: Why don't we just start? Could you give us a little of your early background? Tell us when and where you were born.

Cassity: I was born in January, 1929, at the Baptist Hospital here. My family moved to Forest, Mississippi, when I was four. I went to elementary school there. We moved back to Jackson and I entered the ninth grade at Bailey Junior High School. I graduated from high school here in 1947 and went to Millsaps College here.

Jones: What did your father do?

Cassity: My family on both sides were sawmill people for generations, and we still think that stumps are prettier than trees. I am not a nature poet.

Jones: Was your father from Mississippi?

Cassity: From Louisiana, originally.

Jones: And your mother, I understand, was a violinist.

Cassity: She was, and is, a violinist. She's a charter member of the Jackson Symphony. She was concert mistress for several years.

Jones: Is she still involved?

Cassity: She's still playing. Both my mother and grandmother were musicians in silent movie theatres. My grandmother was a pianist, and my mother, as I said, is a violinist. With the coming of the sound film they claimed to be the first victims of technological unemployment. Al Jolson is a dirty word at our house.

Jones: Was your mother or father either one a strong influence on you as far as your sensibilities?

Cassity: My father died when I was four. I grew up, so to say, in the orchestra pit. I think that that was a very strong influence. I am not a musician myself; I play only the phonograph. I was not forced to take violin lessons, fortunately. I was odd enough as it was. Nevertheless, I think growing up among musicians was an influence, because they all appreciated music as a universal language. That old cliché is true, at least to the extent that music is not a local language. From the first I think that my interests were turned outward to the great world. You cannot be among musicians and not have the sense of an international fraternity.

Jones: So your elders did influence you.

Cassity: Not consciously. For example, my mother does not care at all for opera. As a pit musician she finds the accompaniments uninteresting, and I suppose I myself enjoy the word-setting rather than the music as music.

Jones: You graduated from Millsaps College. You went straight from high school, four years, to Millsaps?

Cassity: Yes. I then went to Stanford for a year. I was then drafted. I thought certainly that it would be off to Korea and farewell, cruel world. But, as a matter of fact, after basic training in Fort Jackson, South Carolina—that dump—I was sent to Puerto Rico for nineteen months and I spent my service lying on the beach under a palm tree. It was marvelous.

Jones: Was that the first time you had been out of the country?

Cassity: No, I had been in Mexico, and after that in Cuba. Well before Castro, I might add.

Jones: Well, I was just trying to establish something because certainly your travels have been a big influence on your poetry. When you went to Stanford, is that where you took your master's degree?

Cassity: Yes. I have a master's in English from Stanford. I was a student of Yvor Winters. Musical influence may have been at work here too: the training given in the writers' programs there was analogous to the strict technical training a musician would get at a good conservatory.

Jones: I was going to touch on that later on in the interview.

Cassity: Conservatory technique is very useful. You may or may not want to use it in every poem.

Jones: I've heard you say that the strictness—the strict meter and the rigid form—is necessary; that you have to have it or you cannot begin to write.

Cassity: People ask me why I write in meter and rhyme, and I can give only one answer: without it nothing comes into my head.

Jones: Is poetry a structure in itself? Does it have to be structured according to formal rules? Is structure, the structure itself, part of the art?

Cassity: You can write in any manner you please if you are not particular what the result sounds like. In the most successful poetry, it seems to me that the structure *is* the art; just as in successful engineering. Not that I have any theoretical objection to free verse, although I myself could not possibly write it. Many free verse poems are interesting and beautiful. Many more are not, of course. And in any event, the reason free verse is popular is that it is easier. That is, it is perceived as being easier. In actuality it is harder. It is much more difficult to write really good free verse than it is to write good metrical verse. The temptation to looseness is too strong. One can remain moral in a bordello, but it is likely to be a struggle.

Jones: In your mind free verse is a lazier approach?

Cassity: Yes. The easiest way to let it all hang out.

Jones: Let's go back to the chronology of your life. When were you at Puerto Rico in the army, in the 1950s?

Cassity: I was drafted in September, 1952, and I was separated from the service in August of 1954. I then took my G. I. Bill and went to the School of Library Service at Columbia University, where I got a degree in 1955. I worked a couple of years at what was then the Jackson Public Library, where I had worked as a student assistant when I was at Millsaps. At the end of the

1950s I went to South Africa and worked for three years
on a South African government contract for the
Transvaal Provincial Library. That's a library system
very much like those large regional libraries in North
Carolina. It's a central facility with which local public
libraries are affiliated.

Jones: How did you get something offered from South
Africa?

Cassity: No one ever believes my story. I was sitting at
my desk at Jackson Public and this gentleman came in
and said, "Would you like to work in the Union of
South Africa?" And I said, "Yes." It had been that sort
of day. He offered me a contract on the spot and I
went.

Jones: Did you have any prior knowledge of the situation in South Africa or what your life there might be
like?

Cassity: I knew if one happened to be the right color
one could live rather well there, which turned out to be
true. I suspect that in Johannesburg, if you happen to
be the right color, you can still live better for less
money than anywhere else in the world.

Jones: And you lived in Johannesburg?

Cassity: I was in Pretoria for ten months and in Johannesburg for nineteen months.

Jones: When did you first feel the pangs of wander-
lust? It's pretty obvious that you were willing to get up
and go.

Cassity: In high school I was very happy here. I had
dozens of friends and a nonstop good time. I went to
Central High. Central was then the only high school in
the city—pardon me, the only white high school in the
city—and the biggest high school in the state. One had
a sense of being very much at the center of things—as
we should now say, of being where the action is. I did
not feel that at Millsaps. One felt very out of things at
Millsaps. It may be a commentary that any environ-

ment in the least intellectual will make you feel out of things in Mississippi. Or, more probably, I was ready to move on. Very soon I was pawing the ground to get to California, as I should think any young man in his right mind would be—as I should think any middle-aged man in his right mind would be. As soon as this interview is over, I am leaving for Palo Alto for eight weeks. Do not misunderstand me. I have no quarrel with the education I received at Millsaps. When I arrived at Stanford, there were no shocking gaps in my preparation. Still, if I had the choice to make again, I'm not sure that is the choice I would make.

Jones: Millsaps?

Cassity: Yes.

Jones: Right. Me too. I felt the same, which is not to forget the many great teachers and friends I met there.

Cassity: I think I simply would have enjoyed a bigger school.

Jones: Did you come back from South Africa to Atlanta?

Cassity: No. I came back from South Africa and worked another year at Jackson Public Library.

Jones: In the 1960s?

Cassity: Yes. The beginning of the 1960s. I then took off to spend six months in Europe, which I hated so much I abandoned it after four and came home without a job. There was a job open at Emory in Atlanta, which I interviewed for and accepted. I went with the thought that I would be there until something more exotic turned up. I'm now completing my eighteenth year there. I would certainly hate to leave. The university has been good to me. I have a very congenial life there.

Jones: Do you ever get to take off in the summers, or a month a year?

Cassity: I have a month vacation and other paid holidays.

Jones: Well, that's good.

Cassity: I wish that when I was younger it had been

possible for me to spend eighteen months or so in the
fantasy world of business. I would have then had all of
the occupational experiences. I would have had the civil
service, the military, the academic. If I had just covered
business, I would have covered all the possibilities. I
suspect there are things that go on in business that I
would not put up with in my office for fifteen minutes.
Business appears to me to be the least business-like of
all the entities.

Jones: When you were growing up, and from your
experience at Millsaps, Mississippi was something you
wanted to get away from? As an influence on your
poetry?

Cassity: Yes, although I can't say it was because I felt
terribly uncomfortable with the then-prevailing injus-
tices, or whatever. I cannot give myself that much
credit. I simply wanted a less sleepy environment.

Jones: Growing up here and majoring in English here,
you must have been at least conscious of the Mississippi
literary tradition, even if it didn't go as far as poetry.

Cassity: Yes, I certainly assumed that it was possible
to become a writer. Writers, for better or for worse,
were blossoming all around one. I can remember when
reviewers thought Speed Lamkin, Eugene Walter, and
Calder Willingham were America's most promising
novelists.

Jones: I heard you say in that interview you did with
ETV that there are only two great novels about the
South. One is *War and Peace* and what is the other?

Cassity: *Buddenbrooks*. When I was in Europe on that
trip which I otherwise disliked so much, I went to
Lübeck, Thomas Mann's home town. When I got
there, I knew exactly where I was: I was in Jackson.
Jackson has a better climate and Lübeck has more interesting architecture, but there are no other differences.

Jones: You mean they are one in their single-
mindedness.

Cassity: In being each a closed, closed world. I am

speaking in the past tense. So far as I am able to judge, Jackson today is an extension of Oklahoma City.

Jones: You weren't influenced at all by Faulkner and what he said about the rise of the redneck in Mississippi?

Cassity: To the extent that Jackson is a city, I am a city boy. I'm sorry, I have never found rural Mississippi or rural anywhere else the least bit interesting. The worldwide influx to the cities suggests that the rurals themselves are in full agreement with me. I also have my reservations about Marse Will. I take a simplistic view of these things. I don't think you can have a great novelist who writes bad prose, and a great deal of that prose is flat-out awful. You can have a great novelist who writes indifferent prose; after all, we presumably have to read Tolstoy in translation. Out and out bad prose I can't take. The prolixity of it! It is the determination of people who ordinarily have no one to converse with to make the telling of the tale take as long as possible. If you want to experience the phrase "captive audience" in its root meaning, go to the courthouse square on a Saturday afternoon. I am speaking of Faulkner's novels. Some of the short stories I admire very much. "Red Leaves" is a wonderful story—the one about the Indian tribe corrupted by slave-owning. That's an extraordinary piece, and it is written in something much closer to textbook prose than those novels that go hundreds of pages with no punctuation. I've often suspected he invented the tape recorder years before anyone else and simply mouthed the things into a microphone.

Jones: What about any of the other Mississippi writers? What do you think about—it may be premature to ask this—the work of such writers as Walker Percy or Ellen Douglas?

Cassity: I find all that very discouraging. Whatever the South was or was not, it was eighty years ago. The latest census shows that less than five percent of the American population now lives "on the land," as those people like to say. Whom are they writing for? There's nobody out there, Massa. The next—dare one hope, the last?—great Southern novel surely will be written about Detroit or Los Angeles or Dayton—Bakersfield, perhaps. Places full of white Southerners who have uprooted themselves and made another life. That's where the interesting South is these days. Bakersfield, for example, is Nashville West. It's a great center for the performance and recording of country and western music. Beyond doubt there's a Southern novel to be written there.

Jones: Don't you agree that at least in the South there's a consciousness of living closer to the heart?

Cassity: Heart of what?

Jones: Closer to an individual's own feelings, because of the family tradition here.

Cassity: No, I don't think that for a moment. The interesting thing about the South, and the one that makes it useful for literary purposes, is true of a middle-class community anywhere. It is the sense of perpetuity, and you can find that in Cincinnati or Milwaukee as easily as you can in Jackson. The middle class is frequently accused of having no ideas, but the middle class has one great idea which makes up for all the others. It is continuity. When you cannot recognize your own life in the life of your grandparents or imagine it in the life of your children, the society is in real trouble. We may be in trouble now. I don't know.

Jones: Your work does reflect an interest in and consciousness of that peculiar Southern phenomenon Huey Long. I enjoyed your poem.

Cassity: I had a great-uncle in the Long regime. I remember when the Watergate scandals broke, all I could think was how very much more interesting Huey and his crooks were than Nixon and his. It is not easy to bring real inspiration to anything as dull as white-collar crime, but Louisiana usually manages to.

Jones: When did you first become aware that you wanted to write poetry? When did you first have the poetic impulse, if there is one?

Cassity: I began by writing verse. I was an anything-but-introverted adolescent, into all sorts of publications and contests and performances, and I learned early on to write verse. Later, when I began to think about saying more serious things, the medium was there. I've been writing since I was fifteen. If I haven't learned by now, I don't think I will, so far as the versification goes.

Jones: What would you point to—a question everybody asks you—as the biggest influence in those early years? What made you write? Was it another writer?

Cassity: For me the great breakthrough came with the realization I was not interested in writing about myself, which, believe me, sets me apart from most other poets, who do not write about anything except themselves. Once I realized that, it was painfully apparent that the great body of English verse consists of poems written in the first person about personal emotions. That is exactly the sort of poetry I am uninterested in writing. There are, need I say, great and beautiful poems written in that way, but it is only a way to write. It seems to me so incredibly narrow. It leaves so much out. How often did you ever read a poem about a bank? Yet think how large a part of our lives economics is. I have written poems about banks, and, though I say it, they are rather good poems. If you cannot make money interesting, you had better give up. However, once you turn away from the first-person lyric, you have to look rather far for models. I found Wallace Stevens a very useful model, in that his poems are full of devices for keeping the poet out of the poem. The poet as narrator, that is. I try to cover maximum ground in minimum space. The poet as narrator occupies a great many lines and contributes nothing.

Jones: That's an interesting parallel. You are a full-time librarian. Wallace Stevens was an insurance salesman, wasn't he?

Cassity: He was not an insurance salesman. He was vice-president of Hartford Accident and Indemnity. I believe bonds were his specialty.

Jones: Both of you, you and Wallace Stevens, wrote while carrying on full-time professions. In your case is it because you needed another profession in order to be a poet?

Cassity: Of course, and not only for financial reasons. Even when I was young, it was obvious to me that the worst poets are those who devote all their time to it. What sort of life have they? What is their contact with the real world? They socialize only with other writers, most of whom certainly are not real, and have in consequence no subject matter. It is true that Wallace Stevens did not write about that insurance company, although, for all I know, some of those poems may be about the Hartford A&I cleverly disguised. I'm sure he could have said some hair-raising things about it. Insofar as his style could not accommodate that sort of thing, it was defective.

Jones: I think what we have to say about today's poets, or about the traditional notion of today's poets, is that they are longhairs playing with coeds on college campuses. I think it is probably true that the best thing you can do if you are a writer is to get the work that is farthest away from writing.

Cassity: That is my feeling, in spite of the fact that there are poets who live rather well. Not on their sales, of course. It is on the teaching and the lecturing, which I am spared. I do not really like to give readings. I do not mind it, and I do it on occasion, but as for filling some emotional need that way, I don't.

Jones: What makes you sit down and write? Is it just a hobby for you, or something you can do well, so you do it?

Cassity: Hobbies are for children and for mental defectives. Poetry is an art. It is *what I do.* I produce poems as a fruit tree produces fruit. Not every year will be vintage, and individual specimens may fail. Nevertheless the crop can be depended on. I pick a subject and see what I can do with it. Obviously some subjects will be more congenial than others and will result in better poems. On the other hand, one should not pick a subject because it is easy to do in the way one writes. That is the way that styles become inbred. I think that is what happened to Wallace Stevens. He wrote about the manner of thing he could write about. I usually try to write happy poems when I am depressed and depressed poems when I am happy. I hope I bring to the writing more detachment that way.

Jones: Is it like a recreation for you, or is it something you have to discipline yourself to do every day?

Cassity: I make no effort to write every day. It's too difficult to crank down at five o'clock and crank back up. I try to reserve my weekends for writing. Fortunately, I never lack for subject matter. You could not explain to me what a writer's block is. If I encountered one, I would sit and wait for it to pass. Writers have writer's blocks for one reason only: they have nothing to say.

Jones: Your poetry seems to have a strong sense of history, of this century's power struggles.

Cassity: I spent the most exhilarating years of my life in the West Indies and South Africa, both of which encompass a great deal of history on a geographical scale that can be managed.

Jones: You said in an ETV interview that those things were not history when you were coming up.

Cassity: I do not date all the way back to the Boer War, but as I said, I predate Castro.

Jones: Why do you pick seemingly remote things for a writer in the South? Why "Manchuria 1931"?

Cassity: I suppose I wrote that somewhat as I might write a science fiction poem. Something exotic and self-contained. What suggested it to me was the von Sternberg film, of which I am very fond—*The Shanghai Express.*

Jones: Have you been there?

Cassity: No, and have no particular desire to go— I might have to make revisions. Ordinarily my research does not let me down. Not a librarian for nothing.

Jones: But in your foreign settings do you see something that reflects your condition or the condition of people around you? why foreign settings at all?

Cassity: You are not going to get me to say something about "the human condition." It is a phrase I do not allow to pass my lips. I shall say instead that we, all of us, find the exotic attractive. What else accounts for the success of William Faulkner? Being turgid as well as exotic, he appeals especially to Germans. If you think that in my youth I was a devoted fan of trashy exotica, you are right.

Jones: Is your art attempting to say something about the world in general, the world as you see it . . .

Cassity: How can the general exist except through the particular? It may not exist at all.

Jones: Faulkner (again) said that the most an artist can hope to do is to reflect certain home truths: certain things that he knows personally, visually.

Cassity: My poetry is full of home truths: avarice, vice, treachery, incompetence . . . good things like that. As for the visual, I should hate to think that as a landscape artist I had to confine myself to Cherokee Heights. Purple azalea against red brick is not my favorite combination.

Jones: What do you see as your function as an artist?

What would you hope that the reader would appreciate in your work?

Cassity: I would hope that the reader would come away with an informed notion of the subject. The poems exist to convey information. May I assume that you know more about Manchuria than you did? Or at least know more about movies about Manchuria.

Jones: I do indeed.

Cassity: I should like to be a disappearing poet. I should hope that after reading my poems through, a reader would not have the least idea what sort of person I am, but would have derived very clear ideas on the places and people I have written about. People ask me if I would like to be famous. I say that I should like for the poems to be very famous, but that I as a person should hate to give up my privacy. I suppose that is asking to have it both ways.

Jones: Have you brought out anything since *Steeplejacks in Babel*?

Cassity: Yes, *Yellow for Peril, Black for Beautiful* came out from Braziller in 1975, and I have a collection just out in Los Angeles called *The Defense of the Sugar Islands*. It's about being in the military in the West Indies. It is from Symposium Press and was published as a luxury item. Symposium is a press devoted to fine printing. The number of people interested in fine printing is small but is probably larger than the number interested in poetry.

Jones: You have written about the black and white situation in South Africa and the Caribbean. Did it ever occur to you to write about it in Jackson? I know you were here in those hard days of the 1950s and early 1960s. Sit-ins took place even at the Jackson Public Library.

Cassity: Especially at the Jackson Public Library. A library presents a much more intellectual image than a lunch counter, and people who are perfectly willing to

deny food on a basis of color may be uncomfortable at
the thought of denying "access to knowledge." I was in
fact working at JPL when the first sit-in took place.
Jones: Then why not write about it?
Cassity: Like much else here, it was genteel and low
key to the point of being a nonevent. Jackson really lets
itself go only for crimes of passion. Poverty and depri-
vation and the ghetto have their place, but for a *truly*
squalid crime, pick a good North Jackson family every
time. The civil rights ambience demands not von Sternberg but a thirties documentary style, and that has been
done to death.
Jones: Have you ever used the people that you knew
and know in Mississippi in your work?
Cassity: Not without changing names to protect the
innocent, if any. I would be the last to deny that the
people you grow up with absolutely form your notions
of what people are. There is no point in pretending I do
not view things from a viewpoint completely Mississippi. Nevertheless, I see no reason to hang my characters over with cornpones like yellow roofing tiles.
Jones: Have you gotten any critical feedback?
Cassity: Reviews have been more favorable than I have
any real right to expect, although I would settle for a
less favorable review if it gave a more accurate indica-
tion of what the poems are actually like. No one knows
better than I do that those are difficult and complicated
poems, but then poetry is a difficult and complicated
art.
Jones: What about your responsibility as an artist? Do
you want the poems to be edifying to the reader's
character? To change lives?
Cassity: Only as all knowledge and vicarious experiences edify. I do not try to improve people. I was raised
a Calvinist and have the great advantage of never being
surprised by the wickedness of the world. Do not allow
them to put on my tombstone that I worked for a

better world because I didn't. There is not going to be a better world. Unless we are careful, there is not going to be one this good.

Jones: It seems to me there has to be something more back there, something to give you the energy to write, other than just to give a small glimpse into certain locations around the world. Most of the reading public doesn't care what Manchuria in 1931 was like.

Cassity: More provincial they. What you say is true, of course. It is one of many things that one simply has to live with. In the last analysis, I regard my art as the most effective way of "telling it like it is," as the phrase now goes, and I live with the knowledge that people who think they want it told like it is, don't. It amused me in the '60s that the "now generation" was so uncomfortable with Brecht. That *is* telling it like it is. At the risk of vanity, I shall say I think of myself as a capitalist Brecht. As you know, the master himself said there is not *that* much to choose. Among other things, he was a very great lyric poet.

Jones: Besides Brecht, whom do you enjoy?

Cassity: Writing in English? Thom Gunn is the best British poet in fifty years. The great loss to American poetry was the death of Louise Bogan. What a hoot to see the feminists taking her up. Better than to have her remain obscure, but I hardly think that her feminism is the point.

Jones: Back to Mississippi. This state is the home of lots of novelists, yet it is hard to remember if there are any poets from Mississippi, unless you count William Alexander Percy. Why is that?

Cassity: I can give very cogent reasons. In the first place, the indigenous tradition is absolutely no help. If there are worse poems than Robert Burns's and Protestant hymns, I don't know them. I like the music of Protestant hymns; it's the text that's bad news. The other point is that the tradition of the garrulous, of the tall tale—which is grist in the mill of any novelist—is no help whatever in poetry. Poetry has to be more succinct than that. You can write very long novels out of the dread Southern urge to use eight words where one will do, and you could write very long poems, but they would be unreadable. Local idioms and local color, if you overdo them, make for instant unreadability and in the long run make for unreadability even if you use them sparingly. I think I can say that in fifty years my poems will be no more obscure than a good deal of currently popular Southern prose. Just try to give some of it to a student at Pasadena High School and see what he makes of it. Pasadena is as highly specialized a place in its way as Jackson in its, but it speaks a beautifully standardized American English without identifiable regional characteristics. I hasten to say that even I will hate to see regional speech disappear, but I remind you that Babel is correctly regarded as a curse. Depending on your bias, you can say that subcultures are entitled to their own language or that the best way to condemn people is out of their own mouths.

Jones: Isn't there a basic American affection for the old home, the folkways, and all that?

Cassity: Yes, and it's why European literature is better than American. There is high art and there is folk art. They are two very different things.

Jones: Have you read Jim Whitehead's *Local Men?*

Cassity: I know Jim. I enjoyed his first book. I have not read *Local Men* yet. I did read a couple of the poems when they appeared in periodicals.

Jones: It seems he's using the old knee-slapping tales in a poetic form.

Cassity: Yes, he needs it. In *The Cossacks* Tolstoy gave us Uncle Eroshka, but he had better sense than to devote the whole book to him.

Jones: Do you know your fellow Atlantan John Stone?

Cassity: Sure.

Jones: Do you like his work?

Cassity: Yes, I do. I think it means something very special to John himself. It's a way of ordering his experience. My observation is that people who do not respect one profession will not respect another. I have no use for people who come up to me and say, "I'm running a filling station, but really I'm a poet." I suspect that what you have there is a not-very-well-run filling station and not-very-well-written poems. John is a very good doctor and a very good poet, and I don't think the relationship is any accident; professionalism is professionalism.

Jones: Do you have anything in the can now?

Cassity: I hate to say it, but when I'm not working eight to five in the office, my mind goes utterly blank. I am now going on leave for ten weeks, and I doubt that I will have a poetic thought. However, I have a great many poems written up that need to be revised and typed, so the time will not be wasted. I find that what I hurt for is clerical time. I have no difficulty in finding or making the time to write. On the other hand, typing, revising, and stuffing envelopes . . . that sort of thing I find depressing. Perhaps I'm too prolific.

Jones: Do you have a secretary?

Cassity: Yes, and that's very helpful. I hate to think what my life would be without my job, and, for that matter, what my poetry would be without my job. I can't imagine a person not wanting to have another profession than writing, if the writing is poetry. I don't see how anyone can write even a very bad novel who cannot bring sustained blocks of time to it, five or six hours a day. That is going to make your economic life very difficult. I think always for a novelist there must be the feeling that, really, you should be able to make a living at it. I certainly never had that delusion about poetry. As I say, working in a library all my life, I know exactly how little poetry is read. It is not possible to be self-deceived.

Jones: Do you gather all the details of your past around you when you write? I hate all these writer's questions, but do you have a routine?

Cassity: No, I sit in a chair in front of the TV set. I am always amused at people who have to have this or that particular arrangement in order to write. If it's that difficult for them, perhaps they're in the wrong art. I really can't say anything very illuminating about my writing simply because it does come so naturally. I've done it so long and so much and, I suppose, too, spontaneously, though I'm sure to most readers those poems seem anything but spontaneous. I can assure them that when I'm writing, I think in meter. It is at least that spontaneous. I'm always amused when the complaint is made that people do not speak in meter. They do! I sit in public places and listen for snatches of metric conversation. You hear them all the time. "The bus is fifteen minutes late today." That scans perfectly. If people did not speak in something very close to meter, it would not be possible to write metric verse at all. The basic mechanical stress of the language is iambic. With the least tinkering, if you have the basic competence, you can turn ordinary conversation into meter that scans perfectly. If it is monotonous, it is not the fault of the meter; it is the fault of the metrist.

Jones: That's true. This is interesting. You're the first poet I've talked with, and it's interesting to observe the terseness with which you talk. Talking with some of the writers, it is interesting to see how their art form shows in their speech. Sometimes it's hard to . . .

Cassity: Shut them up.

Jones: Yes, or get them to speak to the point.

Cassity: They have difficult lives and not much opportunity to express themselves. They just love to beat their gums.

Jones: Well, I do know you've got to get on your way to the Promised Land.

Cassity: Yes. As I said, thirty years ago I was a young

man pawing the ground to get to California, and now I'm a fifty-one-year-old man pawing the ground to get to California. And when I get there, I will be right at home. The last time I was on Santa Monica Boulevard, I noticed that the filling stations, the branch post offices, the street front businesses are all owned by Southerners, white and black.

Jones: Really?

Cassity: Certainly.

Jones: This is in Palo Alto?

Cassity: In Los Angeles.

Jones: Yes.

Cassity: I assume if you had Southerners in Palo Alto they would be agrarians.

Jones: Yes.

Cassity: When people ask if I consider myself a Southern writer, I always say I was born and reared in Jackson, Mississippi; I don't have to go through a charade of being Southern. I am the genuine article. If other people do not consider me a Southern writer, that's their problem, not mine. I must speak very cruelly. I am afraid that what we have in Southern writing now and have had for at least thirty years is the playing out of a purely literary tradition. It's exactly the situation that you had when people were writing mystery stories about English house parties thirty years after there had ceased to be English house parties. It is a purely literary convention that has been prolonged beyond its normal life span. Very soon it will collapse of its own weight. The sort of life it is centered on is, for better or worse, gone.

Jones: But so many Mississippi writers today are turning away from that.

Cassity: Good!

Jones: I can't think of one that still writes about that.

Cassity: Encourage them.

Jones: I really can't think of two more different South-

ern writers than Walker Percy, who comes from a traditional Greenville, Mississippi, aristocratic background,
and Mr. Faulkner. Percy deals with alienation and despair in a modern culture. I think with him and others
it is a new day.

Cassity: My feeling about alienation is, how do you
get it? I could probably use more. To the extent that it
is artistic detachment, I think it is very good.

Jones: Yes.

Cassity: I must not be sanctimonious about Mississippi
and the South. I have money here. The political corrup-
tion is bottomless, but the standard of financial probity
is rather high.

Jones: I'm trying to think of a new novel I've read over
the last five years that really upholds that old tradition.

Cassity: I'll stick with what I said. If these people had
any imagination, they would go to Dayton and Detroit
and Bakersfield and look around and see what those
Southerners are doing. I must tell you that in thirty
years of visiting Los Angeles, I have never met an Okie
who wanted to go back to Oklahoma. For good or for
ill we live in an urban time. It's foolish to turn your
back on it.

Jones: What are you going to do in Palo Alto?

Cassity: Type and revise. I must go. I enjoyed talking
to you.

Jones: I thank you for coming, Mr. Cassity. I hope
we'll have a chance to talk again.